Norwich

The local guide
to a fine city

contents:

about

-

explore

-

Welcome to Norwich

A warm welcome to Norwich; truly "A Fine City"

WE may be biased, but in our eyes Norwich has it all. A beautiful and historic city whose rich heritage continues to inspire our future; here we have an ever-booming independent scene, a strong emphasis on arts and culture and a friendly community spirit.

Surrounded by some of the most stunning scenery in the UK from the beaches to the Broads, and peppered with pubs, restaurants and things to do: it's easy to see why so many people come here, and also why many decide not to leave.

Singing Norwich's praises is one of our favourite things to do, which is why for the past seven years, we've worked towards collating our favourite independent places to eat, drink, play, party, sleep, heal and explore in the city.

Norwich is constantly evolving – meaning we have to as well! This edition is our biggest yet, jam-packed with more of the very best that the city and the wider county has to offer. Designed for all ages and all lengths of stay, whether you've just got here or you've lived here for years; we hope we can introduce you to some new favourite places.

SHHHH

Who we are

SHHHH is a creative collective of Norwich folk brought together through the city and our love for it. We are makers, creators, promoters and proud Norwich-dwellers. Founded over 10 years ago, we've turned our hats to many a venture in that time: creative collaborations, events, clothing – and the *SHHHH Guide to Norwich* is one of our best-known and most-loved projects. We approach each edition armed with different perspectives: some were born here, some moved for work and others blew here on an easterly wind, so between us we like to think we can offer a well-rounded and complete view of our favourite city.

Over time, our ethos has adjusted to face current social and environmental issues. Our aim with these guides and our creative work is to encourage more and more people to embrace their independents and support their locals. That is what fuels us; doing our bit to support others doing theirs.

Map

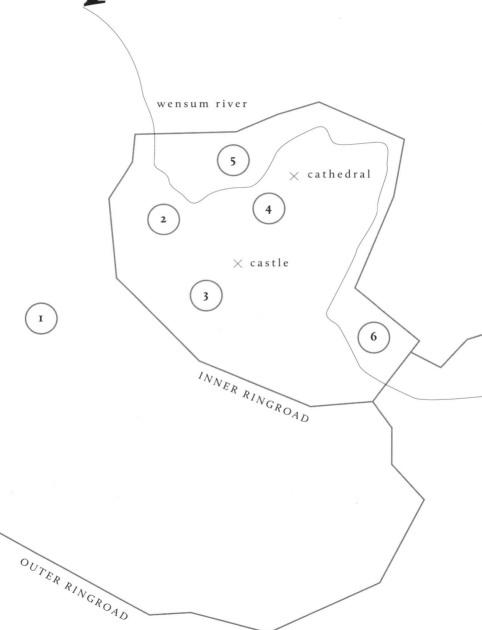

wensum river

5

× cathedral

4

2

× castle

3

1

6

INNER RINGROAD

OUTER RINGROAD

1
GOLDEN TRIANGLE

The Golden Triangle is the traditional heart of Norwich's student community, taking its name from the shape of the area that stretches from Newmarket Road across to Dereham Road. An aesthetically pleasing mix of sloping terraced streets and larger, semi-detached properties, the area's relaxed community atmosphere and plethora of parks and greenery make it one of the most popular places to live.

2
THE LANES

The epicentre of the city's independent business spirit, The Lanes have grown rapidly over the past few years to encompass a significant proportion of the city centre. Representing all manner of outlets, from boutiques to bars, coffee shops to craft stores, The Lanes' charming cobbles have your shopping experience covered.

3
CITY CENTRE

Home to all your chain store shopping needs, Norwich's extensively pedestrianised city centre (get your Alan Partridge jokes out of the way now) also boasts some fantastic architecture, one of the most used libraries in the country and a covered market that has been in existence on its present site for over 900 years.

4
TOMBLAND

One of the most historic areas of Norwich, Tombland is home to the Church of England Cathedral and a variety of restaurants and bars. It's crowning glory is Elm Hill; one of the oldest streets in the city, housing a mecca of antique and book shops.

5
MAGDALEN ST

Just over Fye Bridge from Tombland, Magdalen St is an eclectic mix of international food and clothing outlets, charity shops, antique and book shops, and cafés. It's also home to a cluster of great Indian restaurants and is the starting point for the beautiful riverside walking path.

6
RIVERSIDE

Formally an industrial area, the Riverside development opened in the late 90's and is home to Odeon Cinema, a bowling alley and several restaurants and bars. With the train station at its northern end and the Norwich City football ground at the south, the area is also home to several new housing developments and The Waterfront music venue.

Support your local

THE huge community of independent businesses is part of what makes Norwich so special. From the thriving Norwich Lanes to the ever-increasing selection of independent bars, cafés, restaurants and shops – as a city we are incredibly supportive of each independent venture.

Our SHHHH guide is a celebration of this ever-growing independent scene, with each edition set to capture the community atmosphere, all the while driving new customers to our favourite businesses so they can continue to flourish.

Green City

NORWICH is one of the greenest cities in the country. As well as an abundance of open spaces and the notable green and yellow of our Canary strip, many of us have also chosen to adopt an environmentally friendly way of living.

Norwich has always had a strong Green Party presence, and on a grassroots level the city is bustling with social enterprises geared towards reducing environmental impact. From the 'Norwich Vegans' community to entirely crowd-funded plastic and waste-free shops; there's an evident eco-focused ethos in Norwich. Take a flick through this guide and you'll see just how many of the independent businesses featured pride themselves on being as sustainable as possible.

We at SHHHH strongly believe that 'micro changes the macro' – that individual actions help to constitute major change. Our aim with this guide is to encourage and support more people to bypass corporate or chain businesses in favour of shopping, supporting and connecting locally. Overleaf are just a handful of some of the fantastic schemes that make us so very proud to live here.

Zero Waste Stores

The UK has seen an explosion in the number of independent, zero-waste shops in the past few years, and Norwich is lucky enough to have multiple spots in which to fill up your jars and bottles. Check out The Green Grocers, Rainbow Wholefoods, Re. Source and Ernie's Zero Waste Shop for a restock of pasta, grains, seeds, household products and much more, plus lots of other environmentally friendly products.

Refill Norwich

The average person in the UK will use 150 plastic water bottles annually, but if just one in ten Brits refilled once a week, we'd have 340 million less plastic bottles in circulation. 'Refill' is a grassroots national campaign with a simple objective: to reduce the consumption of plastic bottles by offering accessible water refilling stations city-wide. Download the Refill app to find your nearest spot for when you're out and about!

refill.org.uk

FoodCycle

FoodCycle Norwich gets together every Friday at 7pm at the Friends Meeting House; a merry band of volunteers cook up healthy meals using the surplus ingredients they collect from local suppliers. Since starting in 2011 they've dished up over 8,000 meals, serving over 100 people each week. 'Too many cooks' is never the ethos here: if you fancy getting involved email norwich@foodcycle.org.uk.

foodcycle.org.uk/location/norwich

Farmshare

Farmshare is out to readdress the relationship we have with food; aiming to educate and connect local communities to their produce. A community-owned (CSA) farm based in Whitlingham, they operate a dedicated weekly distribution of organic, seasonal and chemical-free produce to their members city-wide. Regular work days are held at the farm for those wanting to flex their green-fingers and learn more about creating a resilient and low-carbon food supply.

norwichfarmshare.co.uk

Norwich Sharing City

Did you know that Norwich is the UK's first accredited Sharing City? In order to help drive a sustainable economy, solve problems and create new opportunities, Norwich home-grown initiatives such as Farmshare, Norwich Refill and Liftshare are working together to help people share knowledge, goods, services and money. Check out the website to discover local 'sharers' and find out how you can get involved.

norwichsharingcity.co.uk

New U

New U is Norwich's unique swap-shop. Operating as a social enterprise as well as encouraging conscious shopping, it focuses on giving young people skills and confidence by offering retail work experiences in a supportive environment. Instead of cash, a point system is in place: trade your old clothes in for points, and then spend your points on other items in the shop!

Unit 75, 100 Castle Meadow, NR1 3DD

Pure Clean Earth

Pure Clean Earth is a non-profit dedicated to reducing waste pollution around the world through fun and positive events and activities. Volunteers band together to form the 'Trash Tribe', running weekly clean-up sessions, upcycling and talks with a core value of conserving the environment. They're always on the lookout for more Trash Heroes to join the adventure – head to the 'Pure Clean Earth' community group on Facebook to jump on board.

facebook.com/groups/purecleanearthnorfolk

Extinction Rebellion

Extinction Rebellion (or XR) was created in response to the IPCC'S latest report which states that we have a maximum of 12 years to limit the worst effects of climate change. Through large community demonstrations XR aims to ensure transparency on these issues from the government; applying pressure on them to reduce carbon emissions and creating a citizen's assembly to oversee these changes. Join the 'XR Norwich' group on Facebook for more information and to get involved.

facebook.com/xrnorwich

Norwich Natives

AT THE HEART of Norwich lies its community of friendly, supportive and talented people. Artists, influencers, successful business minds and future change-makers will all tell you about the magnetic pull of the city and how it has helped them to further their career and nurture their families.

The Norwich Natives are our hand-picked selection of colourful creators and entrepreneurs – all with different backgrounds, interests and local insights – who have an interesting story to tell.

All photography by Hannah Hutchins.

Henry Jackson Newcomb

IG @henryjacksonnewcomb / henryjacksonnewcomb.co.uk

SUFFOLK born but Norwich bred, Henry became a stalwart of the city's creative scene 10 years ago when he studied Fine Art at NUA. Since graduating, he has continued working from his studio at OUTPOST, exhibiting in the UK as well as internationally. Henry believes in proactively making work happen in the arts to benefit our community; he runs art events with a group of friends through *SAVORR*, and most recently was involved with setting up LOWER.GREEN, a gallery in the much-beloved Anglia Square. Juggling the launch of a new book, a vinyl release, and regular DJ slots, you'll most likely find him at Artel (where he helped design the decor), browsing record shops, or on his lunch break from the studio at Norwich Playhouse or The Bicycle Shop • *sh*

IN THE GUIDE

Adam Peter Hicks

IG @adam.peterhicks / adampeterhicks.com

ONCE a London city-slicker, Adam has embraced the individuality and open-minded nature of Norwich to kickstart his new creative projects. After previously working as a fashion editor at a magazine, Adam has a new t-shirt brand on the horizon alongside his photography, graphic design and styling work. Inspired by the chic of shops like Elm and The Plant Den, he also particularly loves going for drinks with friends in the many bars across the city, as well as keeping abreast of the exhibitions at the Sainsbury Centre for Visual Arts. Adam has found that working in Norwich gives him time to reflect on work. • *sh*

IN THE GUIDE

Elm › p77 — The Plant Den › p95 — Sainsbury Centre › p177

The Burrage Family

theclickdesign.com / nor-folk.com

PROUD Norfolk dwellers and a creative family powerhouse, Bobby and Fiona (alongside their son Stanley) are best known as the faces of design agency The Click and lifestyle business Nor-Folk. Excited by the collaborative creative scene that Norwich cultivates, they have found that work is organically fostered and many clients also become firm friends (and vice versa!). Nor-Folk has just launched The Water Cabin, a new riverside retreat which aims to share the natural beauty of the Norfolk Broads with visitors – a true testament to the love and passion this family has for Norfolk. Catch them spending quality time together at Rabbit, Benedicts and Bread Source. • *sh*

IN THE GUIDE

Lauren Gregory & Simon Sheldrake

IG @crumbagency / @lullabyinc

LAUREN AND SIMON both believe that Norwich breeds creativity; the community's support of new ideas ensures small businesses can thrive. Lauren owns two brilliant boozers in the heart of the city (The Sir Garnet and Birdcage), an events business (Lullaby Inc) and has also recently started a casting agency with a London friend (Crumb Agency). Simon is a partner in a local building surveying practice. When the pair aren't running their various businesses, they can be found having fun with their two children and touring the best attractions that Norwich has to offer; crazy golf at Eaton Park, the magical Plantation Gardens and dinner at the Grosvenor Fish Bar. • *as*

IN THE GUIDE

Marion de Mello Catlin

theshiftnorwich.org.uk / T @marionofnorwich

SOMETHING kept bringing Marion back to Norwich: from moving here with her family in the 70s to art school in the 80s, and now her sense of belonging in the heart of the city's individual, alternative and bolshy spirit! Nowadays, she works in freelance design and communications, is a founding member of Norwich Hackspace, and aims to develop and promote Norwich as a cultural city through two publications, *Art in Norwich* and *Music in Norwich*. Some of the independents she champions include Sistema Norwich and Norwich Puppet Theatre. She credits the city's appeal to its walkability, interesting buildings and an inspiring community that is always ready to connect. • *as*

IN THE GUIDE
Norwich Puppet Theatre › p184

Oa & Greg Hackett

IG @littlelifts_uk / @greg_hackett

AFTER stints at university and working outside of Norwich, Oa and Greg have both returned home to forge illustrious careers. Oa is the founder of littlelifts – a charity which supports women receiving chemotherapy treatment for breast cancer – and Greg is the creative powerhouse behind Spindle, a production company with clients such as Nike and Huawei. They both have incredibly busy working lives and find that Norwich enforces a healthy work/life balance: they live in the countryside with their dog Norma and enjoy walking in the fields and the woods in their spare time. Greg and Oa love the number of independent shops and restaurants in the city, especially in the Lanes. Their top recommended spots include Brick Pizza, Sevenwolves and The Book Hive, and they love to celebrate Norfolk & Norwich Festival each May. • *sh*

IN THE GUIDE

Brick Pizza › p65 — Norwich & Norfolk Festival › p175
littlelifts › p221 — Spindle › p235

Mark Calver

IG @raydiomusic

A SELF-EMPLOYED plasterer by day and a DJ by night, Mark has found that the word-of-mouth nature of the city has allowed his business and interests to thrive over the past 30 years. He currently runs club nights Raydio and Quiet Storm, and is working on a podcast based around Anglia Square and its music history. He loves that Norwich is welcoming to change and is growing as a multicultural community. At the weekend, Mark loves grabbing a cup of tea on the market, walking on Mousehold Heath or spending a chilled Sunday afternoon in The Plasterers. • *sm*

IN THE GUIDE

Michelle Jarrold

jarrold.co.uk

MICHELLE returned to Norwich in her twenties after a spell away learning and travelling. She now works at the family business, where she is currently Development Director and leads on exciting future plans including the celebrations for Jarrolds' upcoming 250th anniversary. Michelle is inspired by Norwich's rich culture and heritage, the beautiful buildings, and the refreshingly modern outlook of its people. She loves browsing the city's wealth of independent restaurants and shops (including Jarrolds, of course!) and some of her favourites include The Granary, Sevenwolves and Farmyard. In her spare time, she sings in Verdi Requiem with Norwich Philharmonic Choir. • *as*

IN THE GUIDE

Nate Revell

IG @gokottahandcraft

NATE is the man behind Gokotta Tailor Shop, a premium denim repair, alteration and customisation service in the city. Born and bred in Norwich, he studied in Cambridge but missed the good vibes and creative backbone of his home. Now, he's looking forward to recording and touring new music with his band and launching a physical shop for Gokotta, where he can continue to spread the ethos of buying well, buying less and repairing where possible. He believes Norwich is the perfect place to grow and master his craft. When he's not working or rehearsing, you'll find Nate at Strangers, Brick Pizza, Drug Store or Tofurei. • *sm*

IN THE GUIDE

Richard Austin

rainbowwholefoods.co.uk

RICHARD established the legendary Rainbow Wholefoods over 40 years ago, after arriving as a student in 1973. He credits his stay in Norwich to the collective character of the city and the creativity, friendliness and helpfulness of its people. Recently, Richard has been busy planning the store's return to its home in Labour In Vain Yard after a fire damaged the premises. He has also developed a selection of successful organic personal care products in collaboration with his daughter Bessie. Richard's recommendations for fun in our fine city include enjoying a drink overlooking the market in the Sir Garnet, visiting the Playhouse and (of course!) a fortnightly visit to Carrow Road. • *as*

Sam & Nic Chapman

IG @pixiwoos

THE HUGELY successful beauty blogging duo Pixiwoo – otherwise known as makeup gurus Sam and Nic – are passionate about all things local and independent. After 12 years in London, they migrated back to their childhood county in search of a friendlier city in which to start a family and continue with their careers. They credit Norwich for empowering them to have a better work-life balance, which allows them to spend more time with their loved ones. Sam and Nic's favourite things to do in the city include summer strolls through Eaton Park, bowling at The Bowling House, plant shopping at The Norfolk Olive Tree Company and celebrating Norwich Pride. The latest exciting Pixiwoo venture has been the announcement of a lipstick collaboration with M.A.C, which will be on counters globally from June 2020. • *as*

Ruth Knapp

IG @Knapple_

BORN raising hell in Norwich, you've surely spotted Ruth Knapp's iconic and bold pineapple tags about the city. Best known for her wickedly unmistakeable murals, Ruth has a permanent gallery at Old Cobblers Café on Park Lane and also helps to promote other local artists through The Underground Gallery (based in the underpass on St Stephens). Drawn to the city because of its proximity to the coast and surrounding countryside, Ruth loves how easy it is to raise her children here whilst also forging her art career. She truly enjoys all that Norwich has to offer – including lunch on Norwich Market, shopping in Catfish and the annual Lord Mayor's Procession. • *sh*

IN THE GUIDE

Joseph Hayes

IG @theillusionofdepth / josephhayes.co.uk

A VISUAL ARTIST who lends his sword to a variety of uses – from creating work for music festivals, musicians and brands to co-running capoeira classes in Norfolk schools – Jo Hayes likes to keep it busy. Creatively energised by the surrounding community of passionate and like-minded artists, Jo has many ventures in the pipeline such as working with new record label 'Curl', a chat show and his ongoing portrait series 'Player Select'. His favourite neighbourhood is the bustling Magdalen St, and some of his favourite haunts include Norwich Playhouse, Cinema City and OUTPOST Gallery. • *sh*

IN THE GUIDE

OUTPOST Gallery › p173 — Norwich Playhouse › p195

Hiroko & Nigel Aono-Billson

IG @kobo_a_b

HIROKO AND NIGEL are the owners of KOBO A–B, a beautiful Japanese antique and vintage textiles, homeware, and living shop on Magdalen St. They moved to Norwich five years ago when Nigel was taken on as a senior design tutor for the Graphic Communication School at Norwich University of the Arts. As residents, they've found the Norwich community to be vibrant, eclectic and open to new concepts, cultures and approaches. This works in their favour as they continue to expand and develop all things related to KOBO A–B, introducing traditional Japanese crafts and makers to the area. In their spare time, you'll find Hiroko and Nigel grabbing coffee from any number of great independent shops in the city, having dinner at Shiki, shopping for interesting items in Looses, enjoying a drink at The Plasterers Arms or at a gig at Norwich Arts Centre. • *sm*

IN THE GUIDE
Shiki › p167 — Norwich Arts Centre › p187

Alice Whitney

creative-nation.co.uk / @creativenation

ALICE is one of the minds behind Creative Nation, a remote content production and creative management agency responsible for some of the most imaginative projects in the city. After 24 years spent studying, living and working across the world, she returned to East Anglia for the big skies, the space and pace of life and the opportunity to explore a variety of exciting creative interests. Alice's favourite spots include Catfish, Norwich Market, the Book Hive and Flint. She loves the city for its walkability, its history and architecture, its outstanding cultural offer and its fiercely independent spirit. • *sm*

IN THE GUIDE

Philip Browne

philipbrownemenswear.co.uk / IG @philipbrownemenswear

PHILIP BROWNE shouldn't require a formal introduction: he's the name (and brain) behind one of the longest standing and most influential menswear stores in the city. Since opening its doors in 1986, he has lived for fashion and still loves engaging with anyone who thinks they know a thing or two about cloth and how its sewn together. Starting your own business might seem like you're asking for trouble, but Philip's optimism, confidence and appetite for risk has led him on a rollercoaster ride to success. His favourite place in the city is Norwich Market, where you'll find him grabbing a bite to eat and soaking up the wit and wisdom from his conversations with stall holders. • *sm*

cafés:

Rabbit

Location

-

6 Pottergate
Norwich NR2 1DS

Contact

-

07940549042
IG @rabbitcoffee.nr2

TACITLY tucked on the Pottergate causeway, Rabbit exudes cosy coffee-and-cake ambience. Rebranded from their former name, 'Roots', Rabbit delights in dark, snug interiors which welcome you from the bustle of the street into the hygge embrace of plants and contemporary ceramics.

Offering a robust menu of sausage rolls and a variety of delectable warm beverages, Rabbit hits the 'lunch treat' spot whilst making all welcome...including our furry dog pals! Relax in the cosy embrace of the plant-laden premises or take your beverage on the go as Rabbit is perfectly situated for those busy city slickers. • *sh*

The Green Grocers Café

Location

-

2-4 Earlham House Shops
Earlham Rd
NR2 3PD

Contact

-

IG @the_greengrocers
thegreengrocers.co.uk

THE GREEN GROCERS is a community café with a menu jam-packed with locally sourced, eco-conscious eats. Offering something for everyone, this café caters for vegetarians, vegans and the gluten free, serving up food that's both delicious and environmentally-friendly.

With coffees made from Strangers' locally sourced beans and over 50 teas to choose from, as well as a selection of organic wines, ciders and local beers on tap, there's bound to be something here to quench your thirst. Dishing up a selection of homemade cakes as well as all day breakfast, including regional specials such as the Norwich, Norfolk and East Anglian plates, The Green Grocers is the perfect spot for brunch, lunch, or any occasion. From sourdough pizza to organic hoppers filled with delicious natural goodness, what's not to love? And with the vegan curry special changing weekly, there'll be plenty of reasons to come back for more. • *gr*

Strangers Coffee Co.

Location
-
Coffee House:
21 Pottergate
NR2 1DS

Roastery:
10 Dove St
NR2 1DE

Contact
-
IG @strangerscoffee
strangerscoffee.com

STRANGERS is an award-winning coffee shop and roastery with two locations in the Norwich Lanes. It's run by three brothers who have spent over a decade learning the skills of the industry, focusing on the quality and ethicality of the coffees they roast and serve.

The café on Pottergate is a great place to sit and watch the world go by with a range of homemade cakes and sandwiches to accompany the choice of different coffees on offer. The Roastery on Dove St is perfect to grab a cup of coffee to take away whilst watching the roaster in action. You can also buy coffee beans from either location or the online shop.

The friendly and knowledgeable staff are on hand to answer all your coffee-related questions. From how to make the perfect cup at home to learning about the different processes involved, they're always happy to help.

Tofurei

Location
-

12 Pottergate
NR2 1DS

Contact
-

tofurei.co.uk
IG @tofurei

SOYA alchemists and tofu producers offering heaps of hand-made vegan fare, Tofurei believe that quality food should be good for the planet, too. That's why they're the only business in the country using East Anglian soya beans to make their tofu. Selling a range of drinks and snacks, from freshly-baked cakes and 'soysage rolls' to kombucha and coffee, this Pottergate-based eatery is a meat-free haven. The ideal spot for a coconut mocha on a winter's day or a whippy-style ice cream in the summer, Tofurei has a vasty selection on offer, catering for all tastes. There's a fully-stocked deli counter with sandwiches, 'soysages' and burgers for the taking – and of course, their signature tofu. Ingredients are freshly made in their Lenwade tofu factory, and products are also available wholesale to a growing number of pubs and cafés across Norfolk. • *gr*

Bread Source

Location
-
93 Upper St Giles St
NR2 1AB

Contact
-
bread-source.co.uk
IG @bread_source

BREAD SOURCE is a contemporary bakery with a deep respect for tradition. Specialising in artisan, additive-free bread and pastries, everything is hand-crafted then slowly baked before being delivered daily to stores across Norfolk. Their shop on Upper St Giles St (and in Aylsham, for those further afield) houses a modern, spacious café serving specialty teas and coffees alongside pastries, both sweet and savoury. Also on offer are baking accessories such as high-quality flour, proving baskets, books, and even aprons for the enthusiastic home baker. Grab a seat in their cosy garden and tuck in to the best coffee and croissants for miles around. • *jc*

Eaton Park Café

Location

-

86 N Park Ave
NR4 7EG

Contact

-

01603 457359
IG @eatonparkcafe

EATON PARK CAFÉ is housed in beautiful rooms at the heart of Eaton Park and offers delicious, homemade brunch, lunch and snacks. There is plenty of seating both indoors and out where guests can enjoy a bacon roll or tea and cake after a walk in the park. The cosy, relaxed and inclusive setting (the cafe is proud to be breastfeeding friendly and welcomes dogs) is only enhanced further by a menu that includes gluten-free, vegetarian and vegan options. The café (run by The Bicycle Shop) serves Sunday roasts in the winter, opens late on select evenings in the summer and is available for weddings and private parties all year round. • *as*

No.33 Café

Location

-

33 Exchange St
NR2 1DP

Contact

-

no33cafe.co.uk
01603 626097

FOR MANY, No 33. is the brunch king of Norwich. For classic dishes like Eggs Benedict, American style pancakes and 'the Big Breakfast', or tasty takes on macaroni cheese, shakshuka or the sweet potato and black bean veggie burger, nowhere comes close for quality and taste. There aren't many places in this vibrant city for which we would be willing to queue, but come Saturday mornings, that's where you'll find us – and it's worth the wait. Make them your first stop after a heavy night out or as a welcome break from shopping...but save some room for those life-changing, doorstop-size cakes! • *jc*

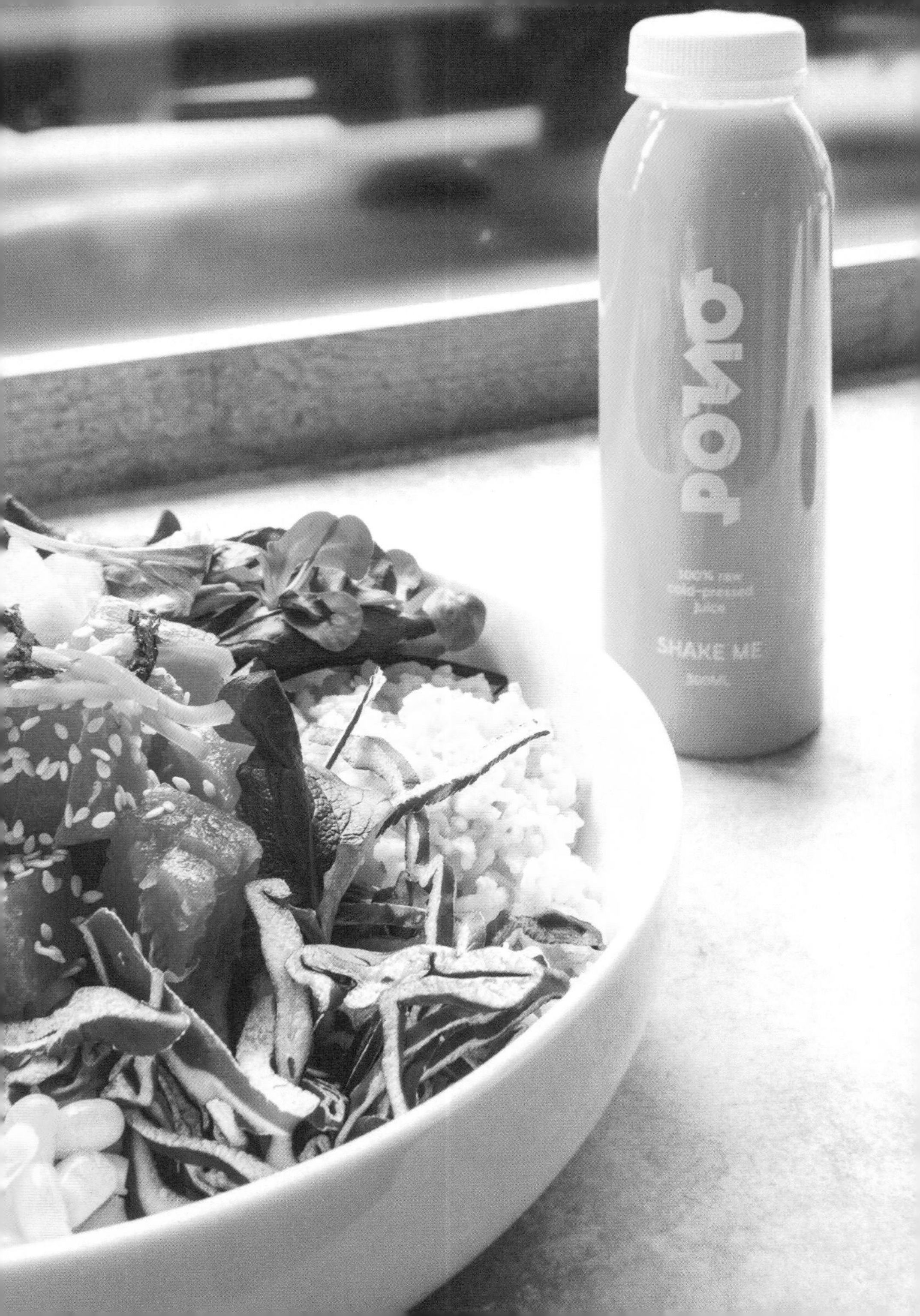
100% raw
cold-pressed
juice
SHAKE ME

PONO

Location
-
15 St Giles St
NR2 1JL

Contact
-
staypono.co.uk
IG @norwichpono

INSPIRED by two years of travelling the globe, founders Ashley and Georgia have been bringing tropical flavour to Norwich since March 2018. PONO, from the Hawaiian word for 'happiness, harmony and balance', is the perfect place to unwind. This superfood bar caters for all diets and appetites, offering nutritious food that's not only bursting with goodness, but with flavour, too! PONO serves bright, feel-good food, like their signature Poké bowls, and uses fresh ingredients in everything they dish up, from customisable salad bowls, to brunch, smoothie bowls and juice. So when you can't decide what to have...why not have it all? • *gr*

The Sanctuary

Location

-

St Alban's Church, Grove Walk
NR1 2QF

Contact

-

01603 477642
sanctuarycoffeestop.com

THE Sanctuary Coffee Stop is a non-profit venture, supporting and raising funds for Norwich's St Alban's Church – whose honourable vision is to be a safe, vibrant and open space for the community. The Sanctuary offers 'outrageous hospitality', with quiet areas and child-friendly spaces, so that even busy parents can rest. Serving top-notch coffee, homemade cakes and buttery pastries, all their volunteers are proud to work together to welcome all as they sit, relax and recharge. • *gr*

The Mitre

Location

-

131 Earlham Rd
NR2 3RF

Contact

-

01603 460512
mitrenorwich.com

A PUBLIC home for the community, The Mitre is a hidden gem in the Golden Triangle, serving up flavourful food and delicious drinks - welcoming one and all through its inviting doors.

Funded by donations and renovated by volunteers, through extraordinary hospitality, toothsome cuisine and top-notch beer, The Mitre is driving change in our region. As part of the STN group, all profits from this Scandinavian style spot fund community projects – transforming lives. • *gr*

Artel

Location

-

67 London St
NR2 1HL

Contact

-

01603 443605
IG @artelstore

ARTEL is what happens when creativity, community and coffee perfectly mix. Starting life as a tiny but perfectly-formed coffee spot on Wensum Street, they've since expanded across a two-storey paradise of great food, great coffee and fantastic attention to detail. Choose from a diverse brunch menu which includes shakshuka, chicken or seitan waffles, tempeh tacos and banana bread, washed down with some of the best coffee you've ever tasted.

The success of Artel's expansion was achieved in part by the team of partners, staff and loyal clients who leapt at the chance to support their favourite coffee spot. The end result is a light and airy space with stunning aesthetics and a bustling and infectiously positive atmosphere. Also boasting a thriving cycle team who run regular social rides, as well as selling handcrafted goods, Artel is a prime spot for a first coffee date, breakfast with friends or a relaxed business meeting. • *tmu*

Alchemista Coffee Co.

Greenhouse Gallery

FANCY a magic caffeine potion? Alchemista Coffee Co boasts a huge range of signature, speciality coffees and coffee cocktails. Rated by the *Independent* as one of the top locations in the UK to enjoy a coffee cocktail, this trendy steampunk-inspired emporium is a gem. Alchemista also offers a great selection of freshly prepared sandwiches, savouries and a wide range of sweet treats. Their sumptuous afternoon teas include traditional, vegan, vegetarian and dairy free options. • *jr*

THE beautiful green-fronted Victorian building on Bethel Street is home to The Greenhouse Gallery, one of Norwich's great hidden treasures. Concern for the planet is at the heart of everything they do, from their natural wine shop and organic café to their second-hand bookshop and the gallery's cutting-edge exhibitions. Previous shows have explored the importance of soil, melting ice, biodiversity, and extraordinary women. Great for local artists. Look out for Tom's excellent wine tastings. • *jc*

Location
4 St Gregorys Alley
NR2 1ER

Location
42 - 46 Bethel St
NR2 1NR

Contact
alchemistacoffee.co.uk
IG @alchemistacoffeeco

Contact
greenhousetrust.co.uk
01603 631007

Urban Jungle

Location

-

Norwich:
Ringland Ln
Old Costessey, NR8 5BG

Suffolk:
London Road, Weston
Beccles, NR34 8TT

Contact

-

urbanjungle.uk.com

WELCOME to Norfolk's own plant paradise! At Urban Jungle, it's easy to lose yourself within a stunning maze of exotic and unusual plants. Boasting a huge range including cacti and succulents, bamboo, trees, climbers and ferns, you'll have a lot of fun wandering through the grass tunnel and rose garden before taking home some plant babies. Plus, the team are friendly, helpful, fully-trained horticulturalists offering a wealth of knowledge on everything they sell.

Shopping can be tiring, so make sure you take a moment to rest in their eco-friendly café which serves freshly-ground coffee, tea, cakes and a varied lunch menu (veggie and vegan included!). • *jr*

The Missing Shoe

Location

-

21 - 23 Castle Meadow
NR1 3DH

Contact

-

01603 850309
missingshoe.org

THE MISSING SHOE can be found in the centre of Castle Meadow, serving up fresh, delicious vegetarian and vegan food by day and tapas-style food by night. Living up to their values of community, kindness and compassion, they host a range of community groups in their spacious building and offer a 'pay it forward' scheme to benefit those in need. They also host the sell-out Hidden History of Norwich Tours – a must-see for anyone keen to explore the underground secrets of our city. • *sm*

Cupcake & Co

Location

-

83 Upper St Giles St
NR2 1AB

Contact

-

07585 443801
IG @cupcakeandco_

IS THERE ever a point in the day when consuming a freshly baked sweet treat isn't a good idea? The answer is clearly no, which is why we're such big fans of the offerings at Cupcake & Co! With a delectable array of cakes of all sizes and savoury pastries on offer throughout the day, you can pop in for a mid-morning pick-me-up (and benefit from their £1 coffee before noon offer in the process) or stop by for something wonderfully indulgent to accompany that afternoon cuppa. With vegan options, larger celebration cakes and all their products using fresh, local ingredients, you're definitely in good company with Cupcake & Co! • *tmu*

Figbar

Location

-

23 St John Maddermarket
NR2 1DN

Contact

-

figbarnorwich.com
IG @figbarnorwich

IF you're looking for the ultimate crescendo to mark the end of your evening, head to Figbar – a dessert-lovers paradise.

The brainchild of Jaime and Stephanie Garbutt, Figbar is an award-winning family business which serves a rotating menu of cakes, financiers, brownies and tarts from early 'til late. The real showstoppers are the seasonal plated desserts, conceived and conjured by Executive Pastry Chef Jaime, who has previously worked with superstar chefs Marcus Wareing and Gordon Ramsey.

The perfect place to grab a pastry and coffee for breakfast, or to catch-up with friends over a glass of wine and something deliciously sweet. • *sm*

Aroma

Location

-

5 Upper King St
NR3 1RL

Contact

-

aromanorwich.co.uk
IG @aromanorwich

DOWN to earth, passionate and – in their own words – sometimes hilariously unprofessional, the Aroma team will brighten your day with excellent coffee and even better chat. The sibling-run café also serves fresh, locally supplied breakfast and lunch alongside a selection of sweet things – including the chocolatiest gluten-free brownies! Experience Aroma in the evenings by attending one of their fun, relaxed events; they host wine tasting, comedy nights, themed parties, private functions and more.

If that isn't reason enough to visit Aroma, their tempting cocktail menu includes the deliciously different Toasted Marshmallow Martini and their famed 2017 winner of Cocktail Week, the Salted Caramel Espresso Martini. • *as*

street food
and take out:

Christophe's Crepes

Location

-

Davey Pl
NR2 1PQ

Contact

-

07581 420352
IG @christophescrepes

LOOKING for handmade, fresh, traditional crepes made with local ingredients and served with a smile? Then head to Christophe's Crepes on Davey Place. Open Monday - Saturday (whatever the weather!), these guys have got every kind of craving covered: whether you've got a super sweet tooth and go all out with their 'UFO Crepe' filled with chocolate and marshmallows, or fancy something savoury like their halloumi, spinach and sundried tomato filling. Your stomach and wallet are destined to leave fully satisfied. • *jr*

Brick Pizza

Location
-
39 Market Pl
NR2 1ND

Contact
-
01603 620661
brick.pizza

DEDICATION is at the heart of everything at Brick Pizza. As they say themselves, 'we do one thing and we do it right', and they're certainly true to their word. From a dough which is cold fermented over 36 hours before being lovingly worked and baked, to their fresh ingredients – cheese from Somerset, meats from Italian suppliers and vegetables and leaves from right here in Norfolk – the love and craftsmanship that goes into every pizza is evident with each delicious bite. With an in-house bar serving Adnams on tap, Brick is the perfect setting to savour pizza, exactly as it should be. • *tmu*

Grosvenor Fish Bar

Location

-

28 Lower Goat Ln
NR2 1EL

Contact

-

01603 625855
fshshop.com

THIS isn't your average fish and chip supper. With a 90-year history of serving up deliciously fishy fare, the team at Grosvenor's have the necessary skill to successfully reimagine our nation's much-loved staple. Offering fresh wraps, zingy sandwiches and spicy tacos made of mackerel, tuna, squid and more, this fish and chip grotto offers everyone's favourite seaside treat as never tasted before.

Family owned and operated, Grosvenor's spacious dining area and relaxed atmosphere invites one and all to savour comfort food at its best. Even offering a 'high sea' alternative to afternoon tea, it's always the perfect occasion to visit Grosvenor. • *gr*

Moorish Falafel

Location

-

17 Lower Goat Ln
NR2 1EL

Contact

-

01603 622250
moorishfalafel.com

MOORISH FALAFEL BAR remains one of the most dependable food destinations in the city, serving up a great selection of vegan treats. Specialising in falafel, you won't be disappointed with a yummy Moorish wrap or salad bowl enhanced with a choice of delicious home-made fillings and sauces. They've recently expanded their menu too, now serving a range of vegan burgers! So if you fancy a treat, come daytime (or Thursday and Friday evenings), this is the place to fill your tummies and be kind to the planet at the same time! Take away or eat in at their gorgeous and cosy upstairs dining room and art space, featuring a new local artist every month.

Take Thai

Location

-

130 Dereham Rd
NR2 3AF

Contact

-

01603 464646
takethai.co.uk

TAKE THAI offers over 65 freshly prepared authentic dishes, cooked by experienced Thai chefs. With restaurant-quality cuisine at takeaway prices, the Take Thai staff cook each dish from scratch and combine quality fresh produce sourced from local suppliers with exotic ingredients imported from Thailand. The tasty menu caters for every diet; over 80% of the menu is available gluten free and there is a vast range of delicious vegetarian and vegan dishes too! • *as*

Fresh

Location

-

Stall 22
Norwich Market
NR3 1ND

Contact

-

IG @norwichfresh

FRESH is located at Stall 22 in the heart of Norwich's bustling market. Selling a wide variety of affordable, freshly squeezed, cold-pressed juices and smoothies, each ingredient is local where possible and chosen with care. Opt for their Matcha Green smoothie for a quick energy boost, or treat your senses to a delicious Strawberry Delight – they always make the perfect blend.

Feeling a little peckish? Fresh also create mouthwatering Fusion Noodle bowls with lots of choices, catering for a range of diets including dairy free. Their products make a great 'grab and go' during your lunch break, or a nutritious energy boost to combat a heavy night out. • *jr*

Voodoo Daddy's &
Rocky Mountain Pizza Project

Location

-

33 Prince of Wales Rd
NR1 1BG

Contact

-

01603 660250

A SHARED VENTURE, Voodoo Daddy's operates in the day and becomes Rocky Mountain Pizza Project by night. Perfectly poised on the bustling thoroughfare of clubs and kebab joints on Princes of Wales Road, this pizza establishment serves slick slices with locally-sourced, gourmet ingredients. Having garnered an excellent reputation for their delicious vegan and vegetarian options, they stand victorious as one of only a few places to offer delivery for a vegan pizza at all times of the day. Serving up rarities such as 'deep fried' pizza and 'the full english', you are sure to find something that satisfies those pizza cravings. • *sh*

Bun Box

Thai Street

GET READY to taste your new lunchtime favourite! Bun Box serves Japanese street food; soft, freshly steamed Hirata buns crammed with a variety of tasty fillings. Their menu is inspired by the East, showcasing fresh ingredients and impressive techniques – from hearty donburi bowls to an impressive rota of daily specials like karaage chicken and dumplings. We recommend the mouth-watering slow roasted pork bun with sriracha mayo, tart green apple and crushed peanuts. • *as*

THAI STREET is a trusted takeaway with something to offer everyone at home. In their previous iteration as Vegan Wok, and with a sister company, Take Thai, serving loyal customers for years, this new venture is a certified hit with meat-eaters, veggies and vegans alike.

Cooking up fresh, delicious Thai street food six days a week, the Thai Street guys are keen to promote healthier eating through their high quality produce and traditional flavours. • *as*

Location
Stall 23, Norwich Market
NR3 1ND

Location
131 Magdalen St
NR3 1NF

Contact
bunbox23@gmail.com
IG @bun_box_

Contact
thaistreet.uk
01603 474747

shopping:

Soundclash

Location

-

28 St Benedicts St
NR2 4AQ

Contact

-

01603 761004
IG @soundclash.records

TRENDS in music can be incredibly fleeting, so it is to Soundclash's immense credit that they remain Norwich's only independent record store – a title they've proudly maintained since opening in 1991.

Every great music city needs a great record store at its beating heart, and owner Paul has fostered a reputation as the go-to person to pick up the latest output from an eclectic range of genres. The loving curation of Soundclash shines from every inch of its intimate interior and should be the first port of call for any music fan in the city. • *tmu*

Elm.

Location

-

5-7 Lower Goat Ln
NR2 1EL

Contact

-

01603 920030
IG @elm.norwich

ELM'S astounding growth as a business since its inception less than two years ago is testament to the time and effort placed on sourcing such a wide range of unique items; something which has helped it rise to the top of the lifestyle shopping market within the city. Having recently relocated to larger premises, Elm's expansion hasn't meant any loss of what makes the business such a joy to visit: a lovingly curated array of contemporary products, housed within a stylish yet welcoming atmosphere. Catering for the discerning design aficionado, Elm does truly have something for all homes; from small press books and original prints, to an extensive range of plants and homewares. Complemented by beautiful ceramics crafted by owner Paige, every home in the fine city is deserving of a fine gift from Elm. • *tmu*

Philip Browne

Location

-

3 Guildhall Hill
NR2 1JH

Contact

-

01603 664886
philipbrownemenswear.co.uk

WITH a striking black storefront on Guildhall Hill, Philip Browne Menswear makes an impression before you've even stepped inside. Once through the door, it's not only the clothes that catch your eye. Alongside the Moncler, Moschino and Kenzo you'll also spy highly sought-after pieces of art. This seamless crossover between art forms is proof of the shop's penchant for creative design that extends far beyond clothing.

Philip Browne boasts a roster of impressive brands. Having stocked early collections from Alexander McQueen and Jean Paul Gaultier in the late 80's, they're early birds for recognising talent in up-and-coming designers. Current stock includes Moncler, Canada Goose, DSquared2, Neil Barrett, Kenzo, Moschino, Versace Collection, Drole de Monsieur, Y-3, Stone Island, adidas Originals, Levi's Vintage Clothing and more. For high-end menswear coupled with stylish, helpful staff, this heritage haven is at the top of the game. • *lc*

The Post Room

Location

-

85 Upper St Giles St
NR2 1AB

Contact

-

01603 470041
IG @postroom85

THE POST ROOM, situated on Upper St Giles, is home to a trove of antique, reclaimed and handmade treasures. Run as a co-operative by four local traders and restorers, the shop is a carefully curated collection of reclaimed furniture, vintage lighting, rugs, handmade textiles and locally-crafted home accessories.

An ode to sustainable consumerism, The Post Room is a uniquely relaxed, inviting shop that beautifully showcases a fine selection of fair-trade, locally produced and preloved items. Framing each object so beautifully inspires customers to furnish their homes with original ceramics, knitwear, fine art and more – all made or restored with love and designed to last. • *as*

Oriental Rugs of Norwich

Location

-

4 Bedford St
NR2 1AR

Contact

-

01603 633520
orientalrugsofnorwich.co.uk

ESTABLISHED in the mid 1980s, Oriental Rugs of Norwich have been supplying handmade pieces for 30 years. Their showrooms are situated over three floors on historic Bedford Street, behind Jarrolds. The staff go to great lengths to ensure they always have new and interesting high quality pieces in stock, with each one handpicked by the company's owner, James Durrant. Many items are sourced from trips overseas to the Middle East, particularly Iran and Pakistan.

Oriental Rugs of Norwich deliver an excellent, professional service, including free home viewings and a unique 'try before you buy' service. • *jr*

Bowhill and Elliott

Location

-

65 London St
NR2 1HL

Contact

-

bowhillandelliott.co.uk
shop@bowhillandelliott.co.uk

A FAMILY-RUN business spanning five generations, Bowhill and Elliott remains a steadfast in men and women's footwear for the city. Proud stockists of Crockett & Jones, Cheaney, Barkers, Loake, Peter Kaiser, Birkenstock, HB Shoes and others, the business also produces its own range of specialist slippers and house shoes from their factory downstairs. Check out their Instagram for their latest lookbook and to find inspiration for your own unique pair of monogrammed slippers! • *sm*

Catfish

Location

-

24 Exchange St
NR2 1AX

Contact

-

01603 619538
IG @catfishwomen

ESTABLISHED in 1992, Catfish womenswear has constantly evolved it's broad demographic of style and taste; showcasing iconic brands such as Vivienne Westwood and Fred Perry, bridged by the contemporary mix of Norse Projects, YMC and Folk and streetwear legends such as Stussy and Carhartt. All of this is threaded together with a carefully curated mix of jewellery, bags and footwear. Situated beneath the concept menswear store Sevenwolves on Exchange Street, together they provide a relaxing and inspiring shopping experience that everyone can enjoy!

Dogfish

Location

-

6 Bedford St
NR2 1AR

Contact

-

01603 762661
IG @ fishmen

DOGFISH has been keeping it real for over 25 years, bringing the freshest emerging street, sport and workwear-inspired brands alongside timeless classics to the city. They are proud stockists of Stussy, Carhartt, Patagonia, Obey, Fred Perry, Nike, Adidas, Nudie and Edwin alongside many others. Situated over three floors on the historic Bedford St, you will find a layer cake of lifestyle, fashion and creativity.

Dogfish's contribution extends further than fashion: their friendly team (part of the Catfish and Sevenwolves family) are integral to the city's creative scene and the store is firmly established as a trusted pillar of music and culture.

Sevenwolves

Location

-

24 Exchange St
NR2 1AX

Contact

-

01603 619538
IG @sevenwolvesmen

SEVENWOLVES' ethos is about providing a blend of lifestyle and fashion conscious wearable menswear, combining wardrobe staples with premium and well-considered design. Sevenwolves are the stockists of a rich mix of collections from Folk, Universal Works, Norse Projects, Oliver Spencer, Deus Ex Machina, Redwing Boots, Camper Footwear and Sandqvist bags among others.

Situated on a corner of Exchange Street in a beautiful former Victorian wine merchants, you'll be greeted by friendly and knowledgeable staff who are on hand to complete this relaxed shopping experience.

Philips Cameras

Location

-

22 Wensum St
NR3 1HY

Contact

-

01603 625261

A DEEP PASSION for photography underpins everything
at Philips Cameras. Whether a professional, an occasional
dabbler, or a complete novice, Philips has got you covered. In
need of a quick fix, a hefty overhaul of your entire setup, or
maybe just a couple of rolls of hard to find film? This is the
place to go. Even popping in to browse is a delight: every inch
is filled with cameras dating back decades, spare parts and
canisters of film. The briefest of stays will probably see you
engaged in conversation about some form of photography and
it's this knowledge and the keenness to pass it on to others that
makes the shop such a joy to return to time and again. • *tmu*

Drug Store

Location

-

8 Pottergate
NR2 1DS

Contact

-

01603 630538
drugstoreskateboarding.com

DRUG STORE is the city's 100% skater owned and operated shop for skateboard enthusiasts. Founded in 2007 by Sam Avery, it's Norwich's one-stop-shop for all of the hardware, apparel and advice you could possibly need.

Drug Store is Norwich's only exclusive stockist of Thrasher, Fucking Awesome, Hockey, Vans Pro Skate, Rip n Dip, Polar Skate Co, Quasi, Anti Hero, Brixton, Heroin and many more. If you're looking for something even more unique, they stock their own DRUG STORE branded goods.

The team are actively involved in the skate community, regularly hosting events and video premieres, and taking a pivotal role in campaigning against a skateboarding ban in the city centre. If you're looking for like-minded people with excellent knowledge of the best local skate spots, or if you don't skate but want to buy nice gear, head over to Pottergate and introduce yourself! • *sm*

The Book Hive

Location

-

53 London St
NR2 1HL

Contact

-

01603 219268
thebookhive.co.uk

PROUD to be crowned the *Daily Telegraph's* best bookshop in the UK and 'Illiberal Bigots' by Michael Gove, The Book Hive is a bookshop unlike any other. With a host of famous admirers, from Stephen Fry to Louis De Bernieres and Ian Macmillan to Eimear McBride, this independent bookshop is a much-loved gem in the heart of Norwich. Explore two sprawling floors, crammed floor to ceiling with fiction, non-fiction, art titles, children's literature, poetry and cookery books; alongside work published under their own imprint, Propolis. Home of the whimsical, the intriguing and the hard to find, The Book Hive also hosts regular events and book launches. The shop's captivating charm and unique browsing experience, curated by lovers of the printed page, simply cannot be found elsewhere. It's no surprise that Margaret Atwood described it as 'eclectic, thoughtful, and tempting – a must for book lovers visiting Norwich.' • *gr*

Design House Norwich

Location

-

31 Timber Hill
NR1 3LA

Contact

-

01603 765553
designhousenorwich.co.uk

DESIGN HOUSE is spread across three floors, housed in a 17th century building in the middle of the sophisticated Timberhill. Amongst the cool interior and exposed beams, the shop boasts premium designer furniture and furnishings such as Christian Lacroix fabric and wallpaper, Vitra and Ligne Roset furniture and Artemide lighting. There are also smaller pieces for sale, such as kitchenware, stationery, clocks and decorative accessories. This makes Design House a perfect place to pick up gifts for others, as well as treating yourself! Whether you're looking for a statement sofa for your home or a new piece of artwork, a visit to this store is an absolute must. • *lg*

Thorns

Location

-

22 Exchange St
NR2 1AT

Contact

-

01603 622891
thornsdiy.com

THE LABYRINTHINE layout of Thorns twists and turns through time, space and DIY supplies, like a black hole that's particularly handy round the home. With more staircases than storeys, stepping into Thorns is an adventure in both DIY and physics.

Thorns has been a hardware haven in Norwich since 1835 (that's older than one of the cathedrals!), catering to enthusiastic amateurs and seasoned pros alike. The friendly, knowledgeable staff are on hand to guide you through the complexities of the store and offer great advice, making a trip to Thorns a genuinely excellent shopping experience. DIY newbie or not, one visit will give you the tools and the skills you need to tackle all those little jobs you've been putting off. • *jm*

The Plant Den

Location

-

88 Upper St Giles St
NR2 1LT

Contact

-

theplantden@gmail.com
theplantden.co.uk

THE Plant Den sell gorgeous, unique and bespoke houseplants, cacti and accessories. Bursting into life as a concession in Jarrold, the lovechild of houseplant enthusiasts Michelle and Roscoe has now expanded into its very own premises on Upper St Giles.

Established in Spring 2018, The Plant Den has quickly grown in popularity and amassed a firm following of both the amateurly green-fingered and seasoned horticulturalists. The range of plants available is fantastic: the Den's varied collections change often, but always offer something for every size of home, office or windowsill. If you can't find the plant you're looking for the team will do their very best to source it for you, and expert advice is always on hand to help buyers take care of their new leafy friends and ensure that they flourish. • *as*

Jarrold Intersport

Location

-

15 - 17 London St
NR2 1JE

Contact

-

01603 697162
jarrold.co.uk

JARROLD INTERSPORT is one of the UK's first Intersport concept stores, offering customers a zoned shopping experience with areas dedicated to running, football, team sports, swimming and more. They also provide customers with a number of specialist services including digital gait analysis, foot scanning, racket restringing and shirt printing, ensuring customers are able to keep both their fitness equipment and bodies in top condition. Jarrold Intersport also houses some of the biggest and best names in workout-wear: brands like adidas, Nike, Asics, New Balance and Speedo.

Knowledgeable, approachable staff are on hand around the store to advise on all aspects of men's and women's fitness and training. Passionate about sports and fitness, many are also part of the Jarrold Run Norwich team – of which Jarrold Intersport is the official retail partner for the annual race. • *as*

Norfolk Yarn

Stiffkey Bathrooms

SITUATED on Pottergate in the much-loved Norwich Lanes is Norfolk Yarn. Owner and founder Rebecca has over 10 years' experience as a yarn trading specialist and provides expert knowledge on knitting, crochet, spinning, weaving and felting. The store prides itself on its diverse range of natural fibres for crafting and its colourful collection of Kaffa Fassett fabrics. For those wanting to learn a new craft, courses are available for beginners right through to more advanced crafters. • *cb*

WHO doesn't dream of a beautiful antique bathroom? Stiffkey Bathrooms have over 25 years of experience in the meticulous restoration and trading of French and English antique furniture. Stepping into their bathroom 'boutique', just a five-minute walk from the city centre, is like walking into a five-star hotel or stately home. Always overflowing with genuine vintage bathroom accessories and reproduction items, you can be sure to find a collection that would look perfect in your home. • *jr*

Location
11 Pottergate
NR2 1DS

Location
89 Upper St Giles St
NR2 1AB

Contact
01603 927034
norfolkyarn.co.uk

Contact
01603 627850
stiffkeybathrooms.com

Imelda's Shoe Boutique

Location

-

1 Guildhall Hill
NR2 1JH

Contact

-

01603 761940
IG @imeldasshoeboutique

LOCATED opposite the Guildhall on the corner of Lower Goat Lane, there's an independent shoe shop unlike any other in Norwich. With it's quirky interior and awe-inspiring window displays, Imelda's Shoe Boutique is hard to miss. Established for 25 years, Imelda's is known for stocking unique, unconventional, high-end footwear brands such as Irregular Choice, Superga, Fly London and Vagabond to name a few, as well as jewellery from Tatty Devine. This is the perfect place for fashionistas after a statement pair of heels! Even if you're not in the market for a pair of Disney-themed Irregular Choice pumps, the beautiful window displays are well worth a peek. • *ejc*

The Granary

Location

-

5 Bedford St
NR2 1AL

Contact

-

01603 697107
jarrold.co.uk

APTLY housed within the sympathetically renovated walls of a Grade II-listed building on Bedford St, The Granary offers cool contemporary home living and furniture. Influenced by Italian and Scandinavian style, the furniture is minimalist modern, casually contoured and unusually upholstered with natural hues and vivid pop-art home accessories. You can find many an eclectic gift or homeware sitting alongside architectural lighting and designer sofas. A branch of the iconic Jarrold store, The Granary maintains its rich heritage and high-class clientele with its collection of mid-century modern and chic wares intended for the perfect contemporary living space. • *sh*

three Magdalen Street

Location

-

3 Magdalen St
NR3 1LE

Contact

-

shop@threemagdalenstreet.co.uk
threemagdalenstreet.co.uk

FOUNDED in Shoreditch in 2001, three magdalen street is a design shop specialising in 20th-century furniture, art and lighting. Their carefully-curated collection includes designers such as Charles Eames, Hans Wegner and Nanna Ditzel as well as contemporary artworks by Patrick Caulfield, Joe Tilson and Peter Blake. With an ever-changing stock and an eye for pristine-original examples, it's worth stopping by regularly to make sure you don't miss out on a key piece from this ever-evolving collection.

In addition to this they stock, iconic Scandinavian pieces made to order, enabling them to work with architects and interior designers on new contemporary projects.

Jarrold

Location

-

1-11 London St
NR2 1JF

Contact

-

01603 660661
jarrold.co.uk

THE JARROLD family name has been at the heart of Norwich life since the 1770s. Steeped in the Jarrold's extensive family history, this grand city centre department store is a much-loved landmark of the Norfolk high street – and has been ever since they first opened their stately doors.

Filled with carefully sourced, curated products, there's always something different to experience at Jarrold. From handpicked fashion and food to books, beauty and exclusive brands, the team at Jarrold focus on the stories – and the people – behind their products.

With three popular restaurants and a well-stocked deli, Jarrold are passionate about good food and drink. From speciality pastas, to fine wines and beers, the friendly Jarrold team doesn't just support local produce but celebrates it.

Offering superior customer service, expert knowledge and years of experience, this independent, family run department store welcomes all – be it to shop, eat or just relax. • *gr*

Rainbow Wholefoods

Location

-

Labour in Vain Yard
Guildhall Hill
NR2 1JD

Contact

-

01603 625560
rainbowwholefoods.co.uk

AT THIS stage, Rainbow Wholefoods can well be considered to have reached 'institution' status; such is the pivotal role that it plays in supplying Norwich's vegetarian and vegan community, as well as anyone else looking for environmentally and ethically-friendly food and household products.

Located in the heart of the Lanes, Rainbow stocks an extensive selection of products, ranging from core cupboard staples to more niche vegetarian and vegan fare, along with supplying customers with a broad selection of other non-food household goods. The first wholefood store in the UK to be certified as completely GM-free, Rainbow have placed quality of both product and service at the heart of what they do for over 40 years...and we hope they're around for at least another 40 more. • *tmu*

The Norfolk Olive Tree Company

Taxi Vintage Clothing

THE NORFOLK OLIVE TREE COMPANY sells a huge range of responsibly sourced, hand-selected olive trees of all different shapes, sizes and ages. Owners Antonia and Paul are RHS award-winning specialists and provide excellent aftercare advice to ensure this hardy, sculptural tree will enhance your garden with year-round colour, impact and interest. Their beautiful show garden also offers palm trees, yucca, agave, large cacti and more - all designed to bring a little Mediterranean sunshine to Norfolk. • *as*

A PURVEYOR of wacky garments and warm smiles, Mark of Taxi Vintage is easily one of the nicest blokes in the city. For us, Norwich Market remains the communal heart of Norwich, and this is where you'll find Taxi's stall selling colourful retro and vintage clothes dating from the 1940s to the early 1990s. Their selection is wide-ranging, with a focus on polyester, cotton, and colour - perfect for festival wear. Tell Mark we sent you! • *jc*

Location
61 Riverside Rd
NR1 1SR

Contact
07766 730893
thenorfolkolivetreecompany.co.uk

Location
Stalls 97 - 99, Rows D and E
Norwich Market, NR2 1NE

Contact
IG @VintageRowNorwich

Coccolino

Langleys Toy Shop

COCCOLINO (or 'little cuddles' in Italian) is a childrenswear boutique offering designer clothes for stylish under-tens. Customers shopping for a special occasion or daytime outfit will find a range of gorgeous brands offering beautiful clothes for babies, young boys and girls. Sourced from the UK and Europe, the shop stocks brands such as Petit Bateau, Emile et Rose, Sarah Louise, Kidiwi and Kite. Coccolino also offers a range of Fairtrade, organic and eco-friendly products • *as*

RENOWNED retailers of all things fun since 1883, Langleys Toy Shop is the place of dreams for kids and adults alike. With a huge selection of toys, model kits and collectables, board games and playthings, Langleys' continuously growing stock (including pre-owned collections) offers entertainment for every occasion. From world-famous names like Lego and Airfix, to tempting classic games and the latest must-have, there's always something magical to be found at Norwich's independent toy haven. • *gr*

Location
25 Timber Hill
NR1 3JZ

Contact
01603 633533
coccolino.co.uk

Location
12-14 The Royal Arcade, NR2 1NQ
34 Gentleman's Walk, NR2 1NA

Contact
01603 621959
langleystoys.com

The Green Grocers Shop

Location

-

2-4 Earlham House Shops
Earlham Rd
NR2 3PD

Contact

-

01603 250 000
thegreengrocers.co.uk

THE GREEN GROCERS is a specialist food store with an emphasis on locally sourced, environmentally friendly, organic and in all ways wholesome products. Expect a wide range of vegetarian and vegan alternatives to animal products, in addition to organic, free-range eggs, local milk, high welfare bacon and the like. Their deli is the stuff of legend and any adventurous home chef will remember being sent here to purchase something off-the-wall and game changing. As Norwich's leading zero-waste store they also offer refills for household cleaning products, beauty produce, nuts, grains and so much more. Bring a bottle and let's work together towards eliminating single-use plastics!

Keep an eye out for the chutneys, preserves, juices, and other homemade, local Norfolk delights from smaller businesses which you won't find in major supermarkets. Their adjoining café – one of our favourite neighbourhood hangouts – has its own entry in the guide. • *jc*

Lisa Angel

Location
-
3 Lower Goat Ln
NR2 1EL

Contact
-
01603 859111
lisaangel.co.uk

VISITING Lisa Angel is like stepping into a treasure trove of thoughtful gifts. Filled with beautiful jewellery, accessories and homeware, you are guaranteed to leave feeling inspired. Looking for something different, something unique? In-store personalisation is on offer seven days a week, helping you to create one-of-a-kind customised gifts.

Based on Lower Goat Lane, Lisa Angel has also expanded to Chapelfield shopping centre – a true testament to their award-winning friendly service and must-have collections. Plus, you can order online for free delivery to store – or order in-store for worldwide delivery! With new stock almost daily, they are well worth a repeat visit. • *jr*

Elements

Location

-

12 Lower Goat Ln
NR2 1EL

Contact

-

01603 618661
elementsclothing.co.uk

ELEMENTS stocks a host of brands in store and online including Farah, Lyle and Scott and Guess Jeans alongside iconic vintage sportswear such as Fila Vintage, Ellesse, Sergio Tacchini. With both friendly, knowledgeable staff and top products on offer, it's no wonder that Elements has received such high acclaim – having been mentioned in numerous publications as one of the nation's finest independent clothing retailers. • *fs*

Aurum

Location

-

21 Bedford St
NR2 1AR

Contact

-

01603 620741
aurumdesign.co.uk

NESTLED in an old merchant's house in the heart of the Norwich Lanes, Aurum is widely regarded as one of the UK's leading contemporary jewellers.

Independent and family run, Aurum showcases some of the most innovative designers from around the world, and is an exclusive stockist of the coveted Marco Bicego and Annamaria Cammilli collections. Renowned for its extensive range of modern silver, men's and fine jewellery, it is also the place to go if you're looking to purchase or design a truly outstanding engagement or wedding ring.

Drawing on their natural eye for good design, the family team has curated a stunning collection of unique contemporary jewellery, with many pieces designed in-house by Charlie. Aurum offers all the services you'd expect from a contemporary jewellery boutique – from bespoke design and repairs, to pearl and bead stringing – all within a relaxed and welcoming setting. • *gr*

Berrys and Grey

Location

-

Online

Contact

-

IG @berrysandgrey

berrysandgrey.co.uk

BERRYS AND GREY is a treasure trove of stylish home accessories and unique gifts. This gorgeous online shop is home to an expertly curated and inspirational collection of designer furniture and vintage statement pieces, all perfect for adding a combination of sleek style and shabby chic beauty to your home. Founder Nicole and her creative team have lent their expert services to some of the most beautiful spaces in the city, including Erpingham House and Mae Cosmetics. Weddings and events are also covered: the shop offers a range of bespoke floral decorations that includes hand-tied bouquets and insta-worthy flower walls, archways and lettering.

From plush velvet furniture and Autentico Chalk Paint to Art Deco gold-framed mirrors; the biggest challenge with Berrys and Grey lies in what to purchase first! Fortunately, the friendly team are on hand to supply interiors wisdom and their 'click and collect' service makes the buying process even more convenient. • *as*

Dipple & Conway

Location

-

19 Castle St
NR2 1PB

Contact

-

01603 626750
dippleconway.co.uk

FOUNDED in 1916, Dipple & Conway Opticians has been providing the people of Norwich with the highest standard of eye care for over 100 years. This family-run business has been passed down through four generations and continues to offer the highest quality service and hospital-level clinical excellence.

A company with traditional values that has no fear of evolving and embracing new technology, Dipple & Conway offers customers the latest and best in optometry. There's also a huge choice of designer frames so customers can look good whilst looking after their eyes; the range even includes unique frames that can't be bought anywhere else. Their highly-trained opticians have a friendly, personal approach – your eye health is their utmost priority.

Dipple & Conway are one of Norfolk's most successful independents with several branches across the region, and it's clear to see why generations of customers have remained loyal. • *as*

Jonathan Trumbull

Location

-

5 St Stephens St
NR1 3QL

Contact

-

01603 629876
jonathantrumbull.co.uk

AN ICONIC thread in the cultural fabric of Norwich high street, Jonathan Trumbull encompasses three locations throughout the city centre. Founded in 1971, the original premises humbly began where it still stands today on St Stephens St, with an increasing demand leading to the opening of Hatters on White Lion St and later the womenswear branch Ginger established on Timberhill. Exhibiting luxe apparel from an array of contemporary fashion houses, they carry a wide range of labels including Burberry, Emporio Armani, Hugo Boss, Maharashi, Persol Eyewear and C.P. Company.

Jonathan Trumbull caters for all occasions, from formal to casual wear, offering a bespoke shopping experience across all three locations with an online catalogue complimenting your in-person visit. Wooden interiors entice you into the St Stephens premises, the ambience is 'understated cool' with the focus remaining on the neatly-styled racks. A true classic in the heart of Norwich's shopping elite. • *sh*

Hatters

Location

-

11 / 13 White Lion St
NR2 1QA

Contact

-

01603 626469
jonathantrumbull.co.uk

HATTERS has been enhancing the wardrobes of Norwich gentlemen with contemporary and classic fashion for just over 40 years. The company's original premises opened on St Stephen's Street in 1971, but quickly needed to expand in order to meet with their popularity and the increasing demand for quality men's fashion that still exists today. Hatters offer discerning customers an impressive range of covetable casual wear; fashionable brands and designer labels include Paul Smith, Jacob Cohen Jeans and Tom Ford Eyewear. The shop also stocks an excellent suit and formal wear range, and with an enviable knowledge of the best cuts, colours and fabrics, Hatters staff are always on hand to aid customers in creating their dream look. • *as*

Ginger

Location

-

35 Timber Hill
NR1 3LA

Contact

-

01603 763158
gingerfashion.co.uk

SITTING pride of place on Timber Hill, Ginger has been offering chic, classic and casual ladies' wear since 1992, with fully-stocked, fashionable collections from high-end designers such as Woolrich, Armani Jeans, Paul Smith, and more.

With style and elegance filling every shelf and rack of this beloved store, Ginger's selection of bags, accessories, jewellery and homeware – as well as lavish Italian handmade chocolates – make the perfect gifts for friends and loved ones alike. This independent boutique also houses a range of exclusive items, including signature velvet 'Love Norfolk' cushions. Whatever the occasion, Ginger adds a touch of glamour to the celebration. • *gr*

Mora Lifestyle

Location

-

95 Upper St Giles St
NR2 1AB

Contact

-

07769 662782
moralifestyle.co.uk

SOFT, soothing textures greet you as you enter the brightly lit Mora Lifestyle. Bringing fresh elegance and a well-audited mix of natural toned furniture, womenswear and accessories, you can find this homely shop-studio on Upper St Giles. Mora Lifestyle endeavours to celebrate organic colour palettes, alongside weathered woods and reclaimed materials. Brands stocked include swedish linen by Nygardsanna, hand-finished silk by Sula and jewellery by french brand Mirabelle. The wares are expertly curated in the space, evoking a casual minimalist decor that feels almost like you have just walked into someone else's living space. Warm, chic and subtly elegant decor for those looking for timeless classics. • *sh*

Head in the Clouds

Location

-

13 Pottergate
NR2 1DS

Contact

-

01603 620479
headintheclouds.com

BOASTING the title of 'Britain's Oldest Headshop', Head in the Clouds sits as familiar as the cobbled churches along Pottergate. Trading in a mystic miasma of colourful handicrafts, bright and beautiful clothing, meditative fragrances and an impressive plethora of paraphernalia since 1971, the shop is nostalgic – if not reminiscent – of a time motivated by peace, love and harmony. Immerse yourself in exotic incense as you as you step into the cosy interior; fantastic fabrics, rolling papers, crystals and jewellery cram every nook, dream catchers and prayer flags dazzle from above. Joyfully celebrating the hippie ethos since their beginning, the shop serves as a community hub, sharing local goings-on and collecting for local charity The Peoples' Picnic. • *sh*

Fords Fish, Fruit and Veg

Location

-

15 Gloucester St
NR2 2DU

Contact

-

01603 622829

IS THERE anything better than fresh, locally-grown fruit and veg? With 30 years' experience, Fords' friendly, family-run business has become an important part of Norwich's Golden Triangle community. Stocking a large selection of high-quality, vibrant fruit and veg alongside fish, herbs, and even logs, coal and kindling, Fords Fishmonger, Fruit and Veg will keep you stocked throughout the year – they even sell gift baskets to order and Christmas trees during the festive season! Plus, they have the added bonus of being environmentally friendly and plastic free, using paper bags to wrap your produce. • *jr*

Dozen Artisan Bakery

Location

-

107 Gloucester St
NR2 2DY

Contact

-

01603 764798
dozenbakery.co.uk

DOZEN houses tradition within its contemporary walls. Baking from 2am each morning, they are proud of the craftsmanship that goes into every sumptuous mouthful. From croissants to their signature sourdough, everything is made using heritage techniques. The open-plan bakery and shop in the heart of the Golden Triangle doesn't just offer some of the finest baked-goods in the region, but everything that goes with them – from cheeses, to chutneys, antipasto and organic oils. Their passionate staff are keen to share their expertise, even suggesting breads to suit your dishes. Artfully handcrafted from simple ingredients, their award-worthy patisserie range is second-to-none! • *gr*

Norwich Art Supplies

WildFolk

ESTABLISHED in 1996, Norwich Art Supplies pride themselves on offering everything artists and craftspeople could dream of. Stocking paints, papers, and drawing materials, as well as handmade pens and oak easels, this is a traditional treasure trove in the heart of the city. Renowned for offering excellent customer service, their welcoming team have the products, tips and tricks you need, whatever your project. From pottery to print making, this charming shop has it all. • *gr*

WILDFOLK offers Norwich field and garden-grown flowers for every occasion. Grower Natalie uses all-natural techniques and traditional methods to ensure that her produce is the best of the bunch – free of nasty chemicals or plastic. WildFolk highlights nature's rustic charm, using foraged flowers and foliage to create arrangements that are full of texture, movement and character. With locally-sourced packaging, everything about WildFolk reflects a passion for the home-grown that you simply can't find on the commercial high street. • *gr*

Location
16 St Benedicts St
NR2 4AG

Contact
01603 620229
norwichartsupplies.co.uk

Location
2 Essex St
NR2 2BL

Contact
IG @wild_flowersnor_folk
wildflowersnorfolk.com

Sew Creative

Location

-

11 St Giles St
NR2 1JL

Contact

-

01603 305888
sewcreative.co.uk

SEW much to see, sew little time! If you are a sewing enthusiast you'll love everything on offer at Sew Creative, stocking a huge range of sewing machines, from basic to top of the range models and accessories to accompany them, plus a colourful array of 100% cotton quilting fabrics, yarns and more. Pop in for a demonstration on any sewing machine or sign up to one of their day workshops for beginner and intermediate sewers. They also offer servicing and repairs on any make of machine, just drop them into the shop for a free estimate. • *jr*

Sir Toby's Beers

Location

-

Stall 182-183
Norwich Market
NR3 1NE

Contact

-

IG @sirtobysbeers
sirtobysbeers.co.uk

SIR TOBY certainly knows his beers. Stop by the store, tucked up in Norwich Market, where every cranny is stocked with the finest craft beers and real ales, plus expert assistance on finding the perfect beer for you.

Aiming to be the principal provider of specialist ales from local breweries, the stock is kept fresh and exciting by weekly rotations. They also offer a 'Norfolk Beer Box' filled with 12 of Norfolk's finest beers which is delivered straight to your door – how's that for service! Using their specialist knowledge, they'll cater to specific tastes for a spot-on selection for yourself, or to make the perfect present. • *ew*

Tombland Books

Location

-

8 Tombland
NR3 1HF

Contact

-

01603 490000
tomblandbookshop.co.uk

FOR over 30 years, Tombland Bookshop have been buying and selling secondhand and antiquarian books from their medieval timber-framed building opposite Norwich Cathedral. Displayed across two and a half floors, the shop has a large and constantly-changing stock of books on almost every subject imaginable: including art, architecture, local history, natural history and music, plus a large stock of specialist and academic books. The experienced and friendly staff also offer valuation, booksearch, book repair and binding services too.

From Bauhaus to Broadland, and Kerouac to Keppler, there is always a perfect book to be found at Tombland.

Ten-eighty

Location

-

6-8 Dove St
NR2 1DE

Contact

-

01603 628123
ten-eighty.co.uk

TEN-EIGHTY is a menswear shop specialising in premium branded sports clothing and accessories. Stocking popular skate, surf and snow brands like Oakley, Fox, Alpinestars, Volcom, Hurley, Element, Reef and Etnies, Ten-eighty offers a huge range of quality designs that span fashion, footwear, swimwear and outdoor gear. The store also offers an impressive range of eyewear, including both sport and lifestyle sunglasses and goggles designed to weather all the elements.

Trading both online and in-store, Ten-eighty has been a firm fixture in the Lanes for over 17 years and has earnt a loyal following of customers from all over the UK. The sales team are experts in the brands they stock, and their friendly, open and approachable demeanour guarantees customers keep coming back season after season. Offering a first-class service coupled with in-depth product knowledge, Ten-eighty is amongst the county's best menswear independents. • *as*

Norwich Market

Location

-

Market Pl
NR2 1ND

Contact

-

01603 213537

STANDING proud in the centre of the city, Norwich Market is one of the oldest outdoor markets in the UK. It's a bustling hub of activity, brimming with a wealth of goods and services including flowers, fresh fruit and veg, clothing, household goods, vintage clothing and more. It's also the most crowded spot in the city at lunchtime; with rows upon rows of street food (fish & chips, falafel, Japanese bao buns and hog roast to name a few) in addition to freshly baked bread, jam and chutneys, cheese, meat and fish.

This year, we were very proud to see the Market officially named as 'The Best in Britain'. Journey into the rows and rows of independent businesses, and you'll see why. • *ew*

The Jade Tree

Location

-

15 Elm Hill
NR3 1HN

Contact

-

01603 664615
thejadetree.co.uk

WANDER down historic Elm Hill and you'll stumble upon The Jade Tree: stockist and champion of our region's finest arts and crafts. With over 20 years' of experience, the team is comprised of five practicing 'in-house' artists whose work can be found in store alongside hand-picked pieces from over 60 other local artists. Each item is handmade and original; from paintings to prints, and cards to fair-trade clothing. Shopping at The Jade Tree is an inimitably personal experience, as the team's clear passion for making and curating art shines through. They're guaranteed to direct you to a special piece you won't find anywhere else. • *ew*

Old Town

Location

-

49 Bull St, Holt
NR25 6HP

Contact

-

01263 710001
old-town.co.uk

LOOKING for high quality, everyday clothing with an individual edge? We heartily recommend a trip to Old Town in Holt; a bustling independent manufacturer of men and womenswear that began life in our own fine city.

Old Town designs an evolving range of everyday clothing that is made to order for each client. Their output is fast but consistently high-quality, producing a staggering 70 garments per week from their workshop using British cottons, woollens and linens wherever possible. A perfect match for those who seek simplicity, functionality and a unique twist on contemporary fashion which makes reference to the past. • *sm*

Elm Hill Craft Shop

Location

-

12 Elm Hill
NR3 1HN

Contact

-

01603 621076
elmhillcraftshop@icloud.com

AT the top of Elm Hill, easily the most picturesque street in Norwich, lives the beautiful Elm Hill Craft Shop. Carefully curated by Christina (who has owned the shop for 40 years), this little treasure trove is filled with an imaginative selection of unusual, stylish gifts for adults including stationery, cards, ceramics, candles, jewellery. There's also traditional toys and wonderful doll's house furniture, books and dolls and more unusual presents including Russian nesting dolls, Beatrix Potter character toys, cut-out dressing dolls and unique ideas for new babies and christenings. Enjoy a meander down the cobbled street and make sure you pop inside for something special. • *sm*

Gallyons Country Clothing

Location

-

7 Bedford St
NR2 1AN

Contact

-

01603 622845
gallyonsclothing.co.uk

WITH two shops in the heart of the city centre, Gallyons Country Clothing is a family-owned business, steeped in history.

Specialising in all things luxury, the Gallyons name has been known in East Anglia since 1784. Whether you are living the country life, or just looking for the country look, Gallyons is certainly well-stocked, with an extensive range for you to choose from. Offering waxed jackets and waterproofs, quality footwear and accessories, stocking big names such as Barbour, Dubarry, Fairfax & Favor, Schoffel – you're sorted, whatever the season.

From traditional tweeds to modern macs, Gallyons houses the full wardrobe for life in the great outdoors and boasts all you could need to prepare for the unpredictable British climate. Smart or casual, come rain or snow, Gallyons are passionate about what they do, helping you find what you need, no matter your style. • *gr*

Yarmouth Oilskins

Location

-

117 South Quay
Great Yarmouth
NR30 3LD

Contact

-

01493 842289
yarmouthoilskins.com

IN THE MARKET for attractive, premium quality workwear? Yarmouth Oilskins have been designing and manufacturing original garments to the highest standard in Great Yarmouth for over 100 years. Occupying the same factory on the quayside and using many of the traditional skills that were refined in their earliest years, their iconic, practical clothing has been re-imagined for the contemporary wearer. Think classic Fisherman's smocks, tunic shirts, single-breasted engineer jackets and one-size-fits-all overalls in khaki, navy, natural and denim.

In the heyday of the herring industry, the business would stay open until 11pm when the Scottish girls arrived to kit themselves out for their arduous task of sorting, gutting and packing the fish. Nowadays, the team of talented machinists and pattern cutters manufacture and supply workwear and chandlery merchandise on and offline throughout the world. • *sm*

days out
and city escapes:

WE LOVE Norwich for its richness of creativity, boundless energy and ability to evolve with the times. But something you don't get with a lot of other cities is its location – Norwich is perfectly placed in the centre of a county rich with beaches, countryside and sprawling sites of historical interest. Just a hop on the train or in the car and you can spend a great day out by the sea, at the zoo, within the grounds of a stately home or absorbing the fresh air at a wildlife and nature reserve. In the following pages, we've handpicked some of our favourite spots in which to escape the city and clear your head.

Parks and Spaces

WHEN the bustle of the city gets too much, it's a relief to know that Norwich has no shortage of beautiful, green open spaces just a short walk from your doorstep. Eaton Park caters for all manner of family activities (tennis, crazy golf and skateboarding included) while Whitlingham and Waterloo Park are great spots for your early-morning run. If you're looking to take things a bit easier, try the Gothic palatial grounds of the Plantation Garden or quiet heathland of Mousehold where you can mingle with lizards, rabbits and deer.

Eaton Park
South Park Ave, NR4 7AZ

Waterloo Park
Angel Rd, NR3 3HX

Mousehold Heath
Heartsease Ln, NR7 9NT

Wensum Park
Drayton Rd, NR3 2DD

Plantation Garden
4 Earlham Rd, NR2 3DB

Marriot's Way
starting at NR2 4UB

Whitlingham Country Park
Trowse, NR14 8TR

Chapelfield Gardens
Chapelfield East, NR2 1NY

North Norfolk and the Broads

TWO of the region's most-treasured destinations. North Norfolk beaches can't be beaten: make a day of it by taking a walk on the Grade II-listed Victorian Pier in Cromer, peruse the antique and craft shops in Wells-Next-the-Sea, then follow the beach round to Holkham, home to the beautiful 18th-century Holkham Hall. Alternatively, idle away the day in the relaxing calm of the Broads National Park before stopping off at one of the great waterside pubs and treating yourself to a well-earned lunch. The Bridge Inn at Acle is highly recommended!

North Norfolk
Cromer
Sheringham
Waxham
Wells-Next-The-Sea
Blakeney
Burnham
Holt
Holkham
Hunstanton

Broads National Park
Salhouse
Acle
Aylsham
Wroxham
Coltishall

visitthebroads.co.uk

East Coast

NOTHING brings a smile to our face quite like the sand, sea and kitschy brilliance of the East Coast. Great Yarmouth is home to the nostalgic Pleasure Beach (our local rival to Blackpool!) as well as an embarrassment of layered histories, from the Time and Tide Museum to the iconic Art Deco Hippodrome. If amusements aren't your thing, try walking alongside the oldest-known footprints outside of Africa in Happisburgh or gain unrivalled access to the Grey Seal colony which calls the Horsey Dunes home.

Great Yarmouth
13 Marine Parade, NR30 2EJ

Winterton-on-Sea
Beach Rd, NR29 4DD

Horsey
Horsey Gap, NR29 4EQ

Hemsby
Beach Rd, NR29 4HS

Happisburgh
Beach Rd, NR12 0PR

Cromer
Runton Rd, NR27 9AT

Caister-on-Sea
Beach Rd, NR30 5HD

Mundesley
Beach Rd, NR11 8BG

restaurants:

Woolf and Social

Location

-

21-23 Nelson St
NR2 4DW

Contact

-

woolfandsocial.co.uk
01603 443658

WITH the aim of providing a new type of eating experience for the city, Woolf and Social embodies foodie luxe with an impressive artisan-inspired menu. The dishes are designed to be shared, with a small plate menu which evolves with the seasons and showcases chef Francis' culinary expertise. Developing from their knowledge of street food and fine dining, the menu marries bougie flavours with the honest sentiment that the 'experience' is all about the socialising. Inside, the ambience is complemented by the modern yet simple decor which utilises repurposed woods and many a plant to maintain an honest, grounded appeal. • *sh*

Pizza at The Green Grocers

Location

-

2-4 Earlham House Shops
Earlham Rd
NR2 3PD

Contact

-

thegreengrocers.co.uk
01603 250000

A HIDDEN GEM in the heart of the Golden Triangle, every Thursday, Friday and Saturday evening the team at The Green Grocers fire up their ovens and open their doors to the pizza lovers of Norwich.

Renowned for its community atmosphere, The Green Grocers offers a staff and service that's second to none. With a range of vegan, vegetarian and allergen-friendly offerings, as well as tasty sides and crispy crusts to die for, this spot welcomes all. Using only locally sourced ingredients on their artisan pizzas, The Green Grocers uses best quality produce to create their distinct, rustic pizzas – all topped with sumptuous mozzarella, or vegan cheese, if you prefer. With their very own organic sourdough bases, slow rising for the ultimate flavour, it's easy to see why their tables book up so fast. And with local craft beer on tap, what better to pair with the perfect pizza? • *gr*

Benedicts

Location

-

9 St Benedicts St
NR2 4PE

Contact

-

IG @restbenedicts
restaurantbenedicts.com

BENEDICTS is the epitome of casual yet sophisticated dining. The decor is comfortable and contemporary, the service and ambiance warm and friendly. The food should not be underestimated: Benedicts was named the *EDP's* Best Restaurant in Norfolk 2016, was awarded three AA Rosettes in 2018 and has been listed in *The Times* Top 100 Restaurants in the UK. Run by chef Richard Bainbridge (2015 winner/2017 veteran judge, BBC's *Great British Menu*) alongside his wife Katja, the seasonal menus feature a wide variety of local ingredients with inventive twists. Menus range from a fantastic value two-course set lunch to an eight-course tasting menu, and there is a Private Dining room (seats 8-16) available for special events. They also offer an exciting programme of cookery demonstrations, so you can be your own masterchef at home! • *as*

The Waffle House

Location

-

39 St Giles St
NR2 1JN

Contact

-

01603 612790
wafflehousenorwich.co.uk

ESTABLISHED 40 years ago, The Waffle House serves cooked-to-order Belgian waffles made with organic, free-range ingredients. Located on St Giles St in a cosy Georgian building surrounded by beautiful architecture, The Waffle House is the perfect place to relax with friends and family. Providing a diverse range of sweet and savoury options, there are some truly unique dishes on offer too – who knew the combination of bolognese and waffles would work so well?! As well as waffles, customers can enjoy Fairtrade coffees and delicious milkshakes made with fresh fruit and ice cream. A Norwich institution, The Waffle House truly has something for everyone. • *ph*

Erpingham House

Location

-

22 Tombland
NR3 1RF

Contact

-

erpinghamhouse.com
IG @erpinghamhouse

PLANT-BASED, plastic and carbon free, Erpingham House provides sumptuous, healthy vegan food that's as good for the planet as it tastes. Next to the Cathedral's Erpingham gate, this charming two-storey café and bar boasts a magnificent pink floral interior (designed by Norwich's own Berrys and Grey) that's guaranteed to impress. The perfect place to watch the world go by, Erpingham House is open seven days a week, from early morning breakfasts to late night cocktails. Whether you're grabbing a turmeric latte to go or sitting down for a three-course romantic meal, you'll find yourself spoilt for choice. • *gr*

The Iron House

Location

-

1 St John Maddermarket
NR2 1DN

Contact

-

01603 763388
theironhouse.co.uk

OPEN for breakfast, lunch, and dinner, The Iron House is an ever-dependable restaurant in the heart of the Lanes. Serving seasonal British and continental dishes with a contemporary twist, the gorgeous building reflects the restaurant's ethos of marrying tradition with innovation. Containing a variety of dining spaces to suit any occasion, the restaurant's chic interior design perfectly complements the building, which has been a pub since 1869. • *jc*

Jive Kitchen and Bar

Location

-

2A Exchange St
NR2 1AT

Contact

-

01603 620330
jivekitchen.co.uk

JIVE KITCHEN AND BAR has been serving tasty tacos, tequila, and takeout since 2016. Inspired by a trip to Mexico, founders Rowan and Lizzie spent weeks cooking up mouth-watering menus in their campervan before finding a more permanent home in their restaurant overlooking the market. The result is an array of authentic and inventive street food; a fiesta of flavour made possible by combining the owners' experiences of Mexican street food and the best local produce. Like the food, the restaurant has a fun and relaxed vibe: diners can book for lunch or dinner, take their meal away or just come for a glass of natural wine and snacks at the bar. • *as*

Les Garrigues

Location

-

81 Upper St Giles St
NR2 1DN

Contact

-

01603 763377
info@lesgarrigues.co.uk

LES GARRIGUES is, quite simply, the best wine bar in
Norwich. Owner Damien has moved from his cosy location
on Maddermarket to the former Louis' Deli on Upper St Giles,
where he has more space to make delicious charcuterie and
French cheese boards to accompany the natural wines he
imports personally from France. Favouring natural wines from
his native Languedoc, Damien's is truly a triumph of regional
food expression – which is why you'll see the Slow Food logo
on his window. The perfect date night if you're sitting in, and
a reliable shop for anyone with even a passing interest in wine.
Don't miss his 'en vrac' (in bulk), where you can buy wine like a
true European; take a container, fill it up, pay for the contents –
better wine for the same as supermarket prices, supporting local
businesses and reducing carbon footprint. A real gateway to the
world of wine. • *jc*

Roger Hickman's

Location

-

79 Upper St Giles St
NR2 1AB

Contact

-

01603 633522
rogerhickmansrestaurant.com

FORMER Michelin-starred chef Roger Hickman's fine dining restaurant serves modern British food in a chic setting. Situated on Upper St Giles St, the interconnecting dining rooms provide comfortable elegance, with welcoming and knowledgeable staff delivering impeccable service.

The restaurant offers high-quality produce with its lunch menu (£20 for two courses, £25 for three), including confit rabbit terrine and mushroom tortellini; and the Table d'Hôte Dinner menu, offering selections such as local asparagus, potato, truffle and smoked egg yolk and braised pork cheek. Diners can also experience a tasting menu (meat and vegetarian), with small plates such as crab, avocado, cucumber and wild puff rice, okra and red onion bhaji. An extensive wine list serves to complement the food, with wine flights offered alongside the tasting menus. With rave reviews, and an AA 3 Rosette Award, booking is recommended for this fine dining establishment. • *cw*

Shiki

Location

-

6 Tombland
NR3 1HE

Contact

-

01603 619262
IG @shiki_norwich

LET the aroma of authentic Japanese cuisine tempt you into Shiki, a family-run restaurant serving sushi lauded by *Guardian* critic Jay Rayner as 'terrific, not just for East Anglia but for anywhere in Britain'.

The restaurant has been welcoming diners for 15 years ('15 years, 15 rings') with a mouthwatering menu that has something for everyone. At Shiki, a meal is an experience; diners are encouraged to eat informally, sharing a selection of dishes so everyone at the table can have a taste. This creates a warm, social atmosphere that is complemented by a contemporary and inviting interior. Head Chef Shun has lived in Norwich for over 25 years and has a masterful knowledge of where to source the best local produce. This, combined with his experience with traditional Japanese cooking techniques, guarantees diners an immersive meal that serves up a slice of authentic Japanese culture in a corner of Norwich. • *as*

Farmyard

Location
-

23 St Benedicts St
NR2 4PF

Contact
-

farmyardrestaurant.com
01603 733188

SOURCING from the wealth of produce the Norfolk countryside and coast has to offer, Farmyard intends to marry succulent homegrown ingredients with top-tier trained chefs. Boasting rich bistro foods cooked over charcoal in an open kitchen, the dining experience is relaxed with a key emphasis on hospitality. Farmyard offers an ever-evolving daily a la carte menu, with set courses for lunch and pre-theatre dining, whilst also catering to all in the Fine City with regular wine pairing dinners and private parties. Open since January 2017, Farmyard offers a contemporary bistro dining experience. • *sh*

Wild Thyme

Location

-

Labour in Vain Yard
Guildhall Hill
NR2 1JD

Contact

-

wildthymenorwich.co.uk
01603 765562

AS INCREASING numbers of people are choosing to adopt vegetarian and vegan diets, so the industry producing these cuisines continues to branch out into fancier (and some would say 'faddy') dishes and trends. However, for every overpriced novelty item arriving on the market, there's still very much a place at the table for those that strive to deliver the key aspects of vegetarian and vegan cooking: freshness, flavour and affordablity. In Wild Thyme, Norwich is blessed with a restaurant that delivers on all three of these fronts.

With a menu packed with delicious, freshly-made dishes, Wild Thyme have been turning out wonderful vegetarian and vegan food for years. Its continued popularity is testament to its success in balancing modern culinary invention with getting the fundamentals absolutely spot on. • *tmu*

Blue Joanna

Location

-

103 Unthank Rd
NR2 2PE

Contact

-

bluejoanna.co.uk
01603 625047

RESPONDING to a demand for more dynamic, global dishes in smaller-plate formats in local neighborhood hangouts, Blue Joanna restaurant and bar has been serving tasty street-style food to hungry residents since 2015. The menu is very timely with Mexican-come-Asian-fusion at its heart. You'll find plenty of miso, soy, sticky ginger, and kimchi on the mercifully short and sweet menu. Vegetarians and vegans are well-catered for, and food represents good value with dishes from as little as £2. A modest wine list complements a selection of craft cocktails and world beers, and events range from live music on Saturday nights to DJs spinning records into the late hours. Don't miss their signature blue corn taco with salsa, slaw, and pickle; and keep an eye out for the blue piano! • *jc*

arts and culture:

OUTPOST Gallery

Location

-

10B Wensum St
NR3 1HR

Contact

-

01603 612428
norwichoutpost.org

TUCKED in to the outskirts of Tombland and turned to face the Cathedral, OUTPOST Gallery melts into the busy hubbub of the city. A dedicated gallery space, it runs on a membership basis, ensuring that the space is committed to artists, by artists. With a keen focus on exhibiting contemporary works, it's uncompromising with its busy schedule of exhibitions throughout the year. Anyone can join as a member and it is encouraged that you submit for artistic opportunities, ensuring that OUTPOST can continue to offer a diverse range of engaging programmes that serve the whole community. • *sh*

Norfolk & Norwich Festival

When

-

May

Contact

-

nnfestival.org.uk
IG @nnfest

THE start of summer is heralded each year by the arrival of the Adnams Spiegeltent in Chapelfield Gardens – a huge structure made of wood, glass and canvas which hosts music, circus, cabaret and late night DJs as part of Norfolk & Norwich Festival. For 17 days each May, NNF transforms the city into an international stage for music, theatre, literature, visual arts, circus, dance and outdoor events, enjoyed by around 70,000 people. As one of the oldest surviving arts festivals in the country with a reputation for innovative and inspirational programming, you're bound to experience something unique that will leave you talking for days. Lyn Gardner from the *Guardian* stated: 'Norfolk & Norwich Festival is now a major player on the British scene'. • *sm*

Sainsbury Centre

Location

-

University of East Anglia
NR4 7TJ

Contact

-

01603 593199
scva.ac.uk

ONE of our top recommendations for a coffee and a browse on a sunny Sunday afternoon, the Sainsbury Centre at the University of East Anglia is a pivotal creative institution for East Anglia and beyond. First conceived after Sir Robert and Lady Sainsbury generously donated their art collection in 1973, it houses a wealth of art and antiquities from different periods and cultures around the world.

The building itself is also a work of art; designed by architect Norman Foster between 1974 - 1976 on the edge of the UEA campus and by the lake, it has become an iconic county landmark. You are greeted by a vast open space with lots of glass and natural light, where the inside and outside run seamlessly into one another. Better still, the Sainsbury Centre has its own Sculpture Park which combines architecture, art and nature in a vast 320-acre space which is free for everyone to enjoy. • *sm*

Norwich University of the Arts

Location

-

Francis House
3 - 7 Redwell St
NR2 4SN

Contact

-

nua.ac.uk
IG @norwichuniarts

A BASTION of education dating back to 1845, the Norwich University of the Arts – or NUA, as we call it – is a home for artists, designers and dynamic creative thinkers. It gives students the opportunity to study in some of the most impressive historic buildings in the city, decked out with the very latest industry-leading tools and technologies, covering arts, design, architecture and media. They also host a range of public events, guest lectures and private views for the rest of the city to enjoy too. No wonder their first chancellor, the late great Sir John Hurt, held it (along with Norwich) so close to his heart. • *jb*

East Gallery at NUA

Location

-

St Andrews St
NR2 4AE

Contact

-

01603 610561
IG @eastgallerynua

THE EAST GALLERY AT NUA is a big part of what makes Norwich such a thriving arts hub. It's a space where the University collaborates with international partners to showcase a groundbreaking programme of contemporary art.

The city centre gallery is home to around six exhibitions a year, with subjects ranging from fashion, photography, fine art, architecture and plenty more. Expect boldly experimental explorations of light, form, structure, and meaning. The best part is that it's accessible to all – the exhibitions are free to enter. • *fs*

Anteros Arts Foundation

Location

-

11-15 Fye Bridge St
NR3 1LJ

Contact

-

IG @anterosarts
anterosfoundation.com

THE ANTEROS ARTS FOUNDATION is a charity for education and the promotion of the arts in Norfolk. From their base in a beautiful Grade II-listed Tudor building, they are champions of the local creative scene and provide an affordable gallery space for Norwich artists. Offering short courses and a Diploma in fine art skills – particularly drawing, painting and sculpture – Anteros classes are led by experienced artists who are dedicated to sharing their skills and knowledge.

Pop by and lose yourself in one of their many books within the growing art reference library, or support their work by hiring a room for a private event, workshop, meeting or even your wedding! • *jr*

Dyad Creative

Contact

-

dyad-creative.com
IG @dyadcreativeduo

DYAD CREATIVE is a Franco-British collaboration founded by Théodora and Hannah, focussing on visual arts and contemporary performance. Exploring what it means to work as an artist, Dyad Creative deliver a range of art projects as well as running creative spaces. Dove St Studios (2015-2019) was an investigation into business models for sustainability and how to support the current artistic community. Over the next 2-3 years Dyad Creative will develop internationally, supported by sector support programme GUILD.

Fairhurst Gallery

Location
-
Bedford St
NR2 1AR

Contact
-
01603 614214
fairhurstgallery.co.uk

TUCKED away in the Lanes, Fairhurst Gallery is a unique space that champions fine art through vibrant, eclectic shows, exhibitions and artist events. The gallery helps to promote both new artists and established practitioners, allowing them to reach new audiences.

The experts in the adjoining workshop specialise in bespoke picture framing and antique frame repairs, restoration and reproduction. Using only the finest conservation grade materials, they combine traditional techniques with contemporary design, and even offer a hanging service. • *as*

Oak Street Circus

Norwich Puppet Theatre

LOOKING for a new hobby or alternative to the gym? You're never too old to run away with the circus! The Oak is the only dedicated circus building in Norwich, home of the Lost in Translation Circus company. With 25 years of experience in the industry, The Oak holds classes in aerial and acrobatics disciplines for all ages and abilities.

Looking to create an event? The Oak's beautiful building and team of creatives will give your occasion that special touch to make it memorable!

NORWICH PUPPET THEATRE introduces the magic of the stage to little ones – and brings adults in on the act too! Situated in a converted medieval church, this unique theatre offers family-orientated puppet shows throughout the school holidays, presenting work from visiting companies as well as their own productions that go on to tour the UK and the world. Plus, children and families can sign-up to puppet making, crafts and animation workshops, and adults can join beginners sessions or masterclasses. • *gr*

Location
St Michael Coslany Church
Oak St, NR3 3AE

Location
St James, Whitefriars
NR3 1TN

Contact
01603 568634
theoakcircuscentre.org

Contact
01603 629921
puppettheatre.co.uk

OPEN

Location

-

20 Bank Plain
NR2 4SF

Contact

-

01603 763111
opennorwich.org.uk

LOCATED in a beautiful Grade II-listed building on Castle Meadow, OPEN is at the heart of Norwich – both in terms of location and culture. Serving as a flexible space for live music, awards nights, gala dinners and conferences, many of the city's best-loved events take place within its walls – including the Norfolk Youth Awards, Norwich Soul Train, Oktoberfest and Corporate Boxing.

The building itself is operated by the OPEN Youth Trust, which uses the profits generated by events held in the building to offer opportunities to disadvantaged young people in the Norfolk area. • *fs*

Norwich Arts Centre

Location

-

51 St Benedicts St
NR2 4PG

Contact

-

01603 660352
norwichartscentre.co.uk

WITH an international reputation for supporting and promoting a plethora of cultural outlets, Norwich Arts Centre is located within a renovated church; a beautiful setting in which to enjoy a range of events and exhibitions. From live music, theatre and dance, to literature, fine art and photography, its eclectic programme of events more than justifies its billing as the best small venue in the UK, a title recognised officially by the *NME*. Registered as having charitable status and with a modus operandi to promote and develop emerging artists, Norwich Arts Centre has something for everyone, whether it be up-and-coming visual artists or Mercury Award-winning musical acts.

Norwich Arts Centre has launched its 40/40 campaign to raise £40,000 for its 40th anniversary in 2020. Visit their website to find out how you can help. • *tmu*

Epic Studios

Location

-

112-114 Magdalen St
NR3 1JD

Contact

-

hello@epic-tv.com
01603 727727

DO YOU LOVE going to gigs, concerts or live sporting events? Look no further than Epic Studios: a fully-customisable venue on Magdalen St that regularly plays host to everything from global household names to intimate sets from local music heroes.

Boasting a state-of-the-art concert-space, including a world-renowned Martin Audio MLA sound system and a profoundly-skilled technical team to boot; the ethos of Epic is firmly focused on pioneering spotless, emphatic acoustics and dazzling optical displays to the delight of artists and gig-goers alike. They're also a dab hand at catering for sports events such as boxing and wrestling, corporate hires such as exhibitions and dinners, and full-spec theatre productions. Make Epic your first choice if you're looking for a space to hire for an event, and follow their socials or check the website regularly for updates on the next live music, sports or theatre experiences coming to the city. • *as*

VisitNorwich

Contact
-
visitnorwich.co.uk

VISITNORWICH is the go-to guide for what's happening in and around Norwich. Part of Norwich Business Improvement District (BID), VisitNorwich markets the city to local, national and international audiences.

The City of Stories is the exciting new brand for Norwich and is a tribute to our literary firsts: England's first UNESCO City of Literature; the first woman to write a book in English; the University of East Anglia (UEA) which pioneered the first Creative Writing MA; and the only National Centre for Writing in the country.

Today, the City of Stories celebrates Norwich's new narrative: a place of unique perspectives, soaring spires and pub fires. A place you don't pass by but go to by choice. From summer 2019, see new branding on wayfinding signs, the printed city map, and on the VisitNorwich website. Look out for seasonal campaigns, and chances to share your Norwich story, too.

City-wide Events and Festivals

Norwich plays host to an array of city-wide festivals and events. Here are some of our favourite annual celebrations.

Open Studios

For 16 days each year, Norfolk & Norwich Open Studios celebrates the county's best artists and their achievements by giving them the opportunity to exhibit, sell and talk about their work. It's the perfect time to discover new art, meet artists and buy original artwork directly from its creator.

May - June | nnopenstudios.org.uk

Head Out Not Home

Fancy an evening out in Norwich this summer? Grab your friends and family and head to the city centre each Thursday for free music and entertainment courtesy of Norwich Business Improvement District. Expect Covent Garden street performers and live music from local bands right in the heart of the city.

Usually July - September | visitnorwich.co.uk

Lord Mayor's Celebration

The second oldest carnival in the UK, the Lord Mayor's Celebration dates back to medieval times. This three-day celebration includes entertainers, fireworks, outdoor stages, a fun fair and lots more. The centrepiece is the procession of fantastic floats, carnival groups, dancers, musicians and acrobats winding their way through the heart of the city.

July | norwich.gov.uk

Pride

Norwich Pride is a celebration of the LGBTQI community for everyone. It's a grass-roots, do-it-yourself party organised by a collective of friendly, creative and enthusiastic volunteers. Established in 2009, it has grown year on year into an inclusive, colourful parade which encourages all friends, family and colleagues to join in the fun!

July | norwichpride.org.uk

Noirwich Crime Writing Festival

Noirwich is the region's largest annual celebration of crime writing and one of the fastest growing literary festivals in the UK. Each year, the world's biggest crime writers – and their fans – converge on the medieval streets of Norwich for a four-day spectacular of readings, Q&A panels, book signings and writing workshops.

September | noirwich.co.uk

Heritage Open Days

England's biggest heritage festival celebrates history, architecture and culture. People can discover local and hidden gems, many of whom open their doors especially for this annual event. There are also lots of experiences to try - from guided walks to theatre performances and glimpses behind the scenes of some of our heritage treasures.

September | heritageopendays.org.uk

Black History Month

A great educational platform for those who know little of, or are curious about African and Caribbean heritage and the connections with Britain. BHM Norfolk's unique flavour draws on a wealth of ancient and current connections which are explored through the many activities taking place – from music to food and even circus cabaret.

October | blackhistorymonth.org.uk

Norwich Film Festival

Rapidly becoming 'one to watch' on the film festival circuit, Norwich Film Festival is committed to showcasing the very best of independent short film. Established in 2009, it's an opportunity to try your hand at filmmaking or watch something different to the usual blockbuster fare.

November | norwichfilmfestival.co.uk

Houghton Festival

Location

-

Houghton Hall
King's Lynn
PE31 6UE

Contact

-

houghtonfestival.co.uk

HOUGHTON has firmly established itself as one of the UK's best festivals – and we're not just biased because it's on our doorstep! Being blessed with a rare 24-hour music license, a reliably formidable line-up, the stunning surroundings of Houghton Hall and a distinct lack of phone service, makes these three days of non-stop festivities an escapist music-lovers' dream. The emphasis is on electronic music, with a mix of genre forerunners and up-and-coming talent, but Houghton also offers a mixed programme including live jazz, dance, yoga lessons and a unique fusion of arts and culture. A truly unmissable highlight of the summer. • *ew*

Norwich Playhouse

Location

-

42 - 58 St Georges St
NR3 1AB

Contact

-

norwichplayhouse.co.uk
IG @norwichplayhouse

AN AWARD-WINNING theatre and much-adored bar, Norwich Playhouse brings fantastic shows to the region, including big-name comedians such as Russell Howard, fabulous fringe productions, brilliant contemporary dance, and fantastic family shows. A firm favourite in the city, the Playhouse is known for its intimate auditorium and friendly atmosphere.

Without a bad seat in the house, you're guaranteed a great evening out at the Playhouse. A trip to the theatre isn't complete without pre or post-show drinks in the ever-popular Playhouse Bar (*p263*), which has a brilliant selection of drinks, a cardboard city on the ceiling, and a riverside terrace.

Wild Paths Festival

Contact

-

IG @wildpathsfestival

WILD PATHS is a multi-venue, city-wide music festival in the heart of Norwich; a weekend of events taking place across all of the city's best-loved music venues, showcasing an eclectic mix of emergent and established artists of national and international notoriety. Alongside the music, there's also Wild Paths-themed after parties, drinks and networking events, live art installations and discussion panels (featuring artists and key figures from the music industry).

Treat your tastebuds at food pop-ups scattered across the festival site and wet your whistle with an exclusive Wild Paths beer, Wild Paths cocktail or even a signature festival roast (coffee). All brought to you by the best local independent retailers.

Wild Paths will take place for the first time in October 2019 – make sure you follow their social accounts for all the latest exciting updates!

National Centre for Writing

Location

-

Dragon Hall
115 - 123 King St
NR1 1QE

Contact

-

01603 877177
nationalcentreforwriting.org.uk

READERS, writers, creators and thinkers are all drawn to the National Centre for Writing. As the front-runners of literary creation, innovation and collaboration both in the city and around the world, their role is to explore how writing can inspire, challenge and change the world we live in.

Based in the historic Dragon Hall – a medieval building with more than a few stories of itself to tell – their year-round programme includes workshops for aspiring writers, festival events with cutting-edge authors and outreach projects for schools and community groups. In short, it is a place for everyone who loves words and the stories woven from them. • *sm*

Norfolk Enterprise Festival

Location 2019

-

Hoveton Hall
NR12 8RJ

Contact

-

admin@norfolkenterprisefestival.co.uk
norfolkenterprisefestival.co.uk

THE NORFOLK ENTERPRISE FESTIVAL is an annual gathering of the county's entrepreneurs, startups, SMEs and investors. This not-for-profit event is a place for like-minded business people to connect, celebrate and learn from each other.

Attendees can be inspired by motivating talks, interactive workshops and expert panels. Also on offer are valuable free one-to-one business advice sessions and the opportunity to network with investment angels. The festival is designed to be inclusive and family friendly, offering creative workshops, homegrown musicians and entertaining theatre shows. All this, paired with local food and drink, guarantees a fun, inspirational day out for everyone involved. • *as*

The Maddermarket Theatre

Location
-
St John's Alley
NR2 1DR

Contact
-
01603 620917
maddermarket.co.uk

TUCKED up behind Pottergate, the historic Maddermarket Theatre has been hosting theatrics since 1921. These days, the theatre is renowned for its exceptionally-varied programming; from classical opera to contemporary musical showcases, stand-up comedy, dance, theatre productions and talks, their three performance spaces showcase their versatility throughout the year. The Maddermarket team's passion for theatre extends to more than hosting: they produce eleven in-house shows a year and nurture youth theatre with a busy programme of classes and workshops. Be sure to check out the bar, stocked with locally-brewed Adnams beers, pre-show – or hang out afterwards to catch the performers enjoying a well-deserved drink. • *ew*

Mandell's Gallery

Location

-

Elm Hill
NR3 1HN

Contact

-

01603 626892
mandellsgallery.co.uk

NESTLED amidst the historic cobbles of Elm Hill, Mandell's Gallery showcases a dynamic range of contemporary and traditional art.

Founded in 1965, Mandell's originally specialised in works by the prolific 19th-century Norwich School painters. Since then, the gallery has expanded and now houses a variety of art in beautifully curated collections and exhibitions that date from 1800 to the present day. Both continental and English art is displayed, with an emphasis on work from local practitioners. Exhibitions change every four weeks, so there is always exciting new work to see, and the gallery's friendly, knowledgeable staff are always on hand to offer help and guidance. • *as*

Pizza Club Promotions

SAVORR

PIZZA CLUB are out to deliver a fresh slice of live music to Norwich! Founded by Ben Street, this collective of promoters, designers and event organisers have been working hard to put on spectacular live shows with nationally-renowned artists as well as, crucially, supporting up-and-coming local musicians.

Showcasing an eclectic range of music, the collective has big plans for their future projects; including multimedia displays, art exhibits, pop-up stalls and (obviously!) pizza. • *ew*

SAVORR is a non-profit, independent arts organisation based in Norwich with no fixed gallery or location. Since its launch in 2011, *SAVORR* has worked with over 200 artists from the UK and internationally across 20 exhibitions and events.

Join them for *SAVORR SOCIAL*, a series of events showcasing new and engaging work, also offering a regular place for people to meet. Sign up to their mailing list to hear about new opportunities and events.

Contact
pizzaclubpromo.eventbrite.co.uk
IG @pizzaclubpromo

Contact
savorr.co.uk
IG @savorr_

The South Asia Collection

Location

-

34-36 Bethel St
NR2 1NR

Contact

-

thesouthasiacollection.co.uk
IG @thesouthasiacollection

THE South Asia Collection celebrates the arts, crafts and cultures of South Asia and neighbouring countries. The diverse collection is housed in a beautifully restored Victorian roller skating rink – an unusual setting that complements the rich history of each artefact. From intricately embroidered Kutchi camel covers to 19th-century views of the Himalayas, or carved architecture from Lahore, every object tells a fascinating story.

The museum was founded by Philip and Jeannie Millward, who began the collection in 1979. Along with the South Asian Decorative Arts and Crafts Collection Trust (SADACC) they work hard to conserve and promote the traditional arts and crafts of South Asia. The South Asia Collection shop, run by Country & Eastern, offers a unique range of objects and textiles direct from makers in South Asia. • *as*

The Forum

Location

-

Millennium Plain

NR2 1TF

Contact

-

01603 727950

theforumnorwich.co.uk

THE huge glass fronted Forum, located in the centre of Norwich, is one of the city's most spectacular landmarks.

Open seven days a week, there's always something to see and do with thousands of people passing through every day. The Forum is run by an independent, self-financing charity, The Forum Trust, which runs a year-round programme of free events and activities; including Norwich Games Festival, Norfolk Makers' Festival and Norwich Science Festival.

The building is also home to one of the busiest libraries in the country, along with Pizza Express, Café Bar Marzano and the BBC Look East studios.

Future Radio

Location
-
20 Bank Plain
NR2 4SF

Contact
-
01603 250056
futureradio.co.uk

THE voice of our fine city, Future Radio is one of the largest and longest running community radio stations in the UK. It's a radio station run for, and by, the community, offering anyone and everyone the opportunity to get involved; whether it is creating their own radio show, assisting with background production or developing their skills in journalism. They also fully support local bands and singer-songwriters, giving them the perfect platform to express their creativity. So whether you're tuning in, turning up, or both, the future of radio in Norwich is bright. • *jr*

Promoters

A musical community and bi-monthly get together, Parish focuses on forward-thinking selections and creating high-energy dance floors. Local talents soundtrack the dance, alongside some exciting headline artists from further afield. Promoting inclusivity in both crowd and sound, Parish moves across house, disco, techno and soul with influences from around the world. Dancing strictly encouraged!

@norwichparish

'Music for lovers' is Raydio's ethos. True lovers of music in the broadest sense, Raydio has a loose focus on genre, choosing instead to spin an eclectic assortment of soul, house, techno, Afro/Tropical, jazz and hip-hop played with affection, every time. They recently celebrated two years of bringing a mixed crowd together over proper tunes – and we're hoping for many more!

@raydiomusic

Bunk have been a constant, trusted and above all fun fixture in Norwich nightlife for over five years. They've thrown parties at all our city's notable venues (including an open-air bus!) and are now settled into their new home at Bermuda Bob's. Bunk's residents have been finessing their trademark blend of disco, house and techno for years, and more recently they've started turning their attention towards bringing in some stellar bookings.

@bunkcollective

Soul Stew provide genre-defying dance floor sounds from all over the world. Their vinyl-only parties focus on creating an inclusive dance space for music lovers, inviting some of the world's most respected 'crate diggers' to play - including Mark Grusane, Sadar Bahar, Volcov and Charlie Bones. Events have also expanded to include talks, collaborative parties and the ever-popular 'Bowl Stew' – pairing bowling with a boogie!

@soulstew | @soulfulstew

All Shapes play music to make you dance...pure and simple. A proper community project, the collective began with some notorious local parties, but are now taking their brand of feel-good, unpretentious party-purveying and opening it up for the whole city to enjoy. Keep your eyes peeled for the next date and don't miss out.

@_allshapes

A DJ who strives to dig deeper, Chanelle One provides 'journeys into disco and boogie' via a giant helping of lost and forgotten disco, alongside uplifting house gems. Make sure you follow their social channels where musical discoveries are posted regularly, as well as details for when and where you can jump onto the next Chanelle One adventure.

@chanelle_one_disco

If you're looking for a proper party, look out for YAYA. Dale, Lee and Stu have been running the popular collective for over five years, with a signature focus on deep and minimal sounds. The trio also play together as PRiiMO, run their own record label YAYA Records, and venture both nationally and worldwide. You'll find them in Norwich at their trusted home, Gonzo's Tea Room.

@yayanights

Thomas and Vialli like to do things a little differently, throwing parties in both Norwich and London with a simple ethos: 'late night sounds and XXL feelings'. Think dancefloor-destined selections, often accompanied by art installations, and a trademark escapist atmosphere. Always high-energy and always fun, party-goers are strongly encouraged to leave any preconceptions at the door and commit to the dance!

@rowgdeparture

made in norwich:

Carol Lake Studio

Location

-

91 Upper St Giles St
NR2 1AB

Contact

-

07736 731338
IG @carollakedesigner

STEPPING into the studio space of designer Carol Lake is like entering a botanical paradise. The shop displays a beautifully-curated selection of Carol's framed, floral-inspired artwork, alongside products like scarves, cushions, robes and fabric by the metre. Each design starts life as a piece of Carol's original hand-painted work, and is adapted into a covetable object of beauty. Alongside her own wares, Carol also stocks a small collection of botanically-inspired products from other makers. In 2019, the studio will be hosting a series of pop-up tearooms, which will feature Carol working alongside a wonderful cook to offer guests a blossoming dining experience. • *as*

Norridge

Lennie Beare

PORRIDGE might well be our favourite breakfast food of choice – and it certainly served as the blossoming point for Rowan and Liv's friendship. Their mutual love of porridge, combined with their shared interest in slow living and seasonal eating has developed into what is now known as 'Norridge'; a unique series of porridge pop-up events that stand to encourage a nourishing and considered lifestyle for Norwich city dwellers. Since their first pop-up weekend, Norridge has extended into wellbeing and yoga events and ethically-made merchandise. The creative duo are also available for design and photography jobs and extremely satisfying event catering. • *ew*

Contact
IG @norridge.popup
norridgepopup@gmail.com

LENNIE Beare has been designing and hand-making contemporary jewellery with character since 2015. Using a unique combination of traditional making skills with free-hand drawing, Lennie's jewellery is bold, elegant and stylish: timeless designs for years of wear to come. Allowing the process of making to dictate the final shape makes each wedding ring, earring or necklace totally one-of-a-kind. Lennie's plant-filled city centre studio is open by appointment or at regular open studio events.

Location
Lion House Studios, Muspole St
NR3 1DJ

Contact
lenniebeare.com
IG @lenniebeare

The Foreign Locals

Todd Designs

PIRATE Joe and the Foreign Locals are true entertainers. Brought together through busking on the streets of Norwich, the band – guitar, accordion and drums plus frontman Pirate Joe – really know how to pull a crowd. Their boundless energy is infectious as they deliver high-energy original tunes influenced by everything from gypsy folk to raving dance tracks. They've played extensively throughout the county, produced an album together and, under all their energy and showmanship, are a seriously musically talented bunch. • *ew*

RUEFUL of the barrage of waste we each find ourselves collecting, David Todd uses his skillful eye and canny ability to concoct a myriad of repurposed items, such as lamps, storage containers and furniture. All of his projects use upcycled materials in a bid to bring a new connection to objects considered disposable. Each item's design is informed by the components it is made from, ensuring that each piece is truly one-of-a-kind. • *sh*

Location
59 St Augustines St
NR3 3BG

Contact
aceprodutions@outlook.com
FB/PJandtheFLs

Contact
todddesigns.co.uk
IG @todddesigns_

Nor–Folk

Contact

-

nor-folk.com
IG @nor_folk

NOR–FOLK is a design-led lifestyle brand, comprising a journal, creative studio and online store led by creative director, Fiona Burrage. The 'Nor–Folk' way of life is about living deliberately; about doing something once and doing it well.

Browse the online journal and you'll find design and lifestyle inspiration; from interiors, fashion, business and travel, to food and beauty. You'll also catch a glimpse into the Nor-Folk family life – with Fiona, her husband, Bobby, and son Stanley, at home and on their travels.

Nor-Folk's online store is home to their iconic quality apparel and homewares – simple, minimal items that stand the test of time. You can share Nor-Folk's journey of 'designing a simpler life' online and via their social media channels. • *lt*

Liam Ashley Clark

Sam Harrons

SINCE graduating from NUA, Liam Ashley Clark has been finessing and showcasing his now trademark artistic style. His work is infused with bright colours, influenced by DIY and skate culture, politics, hip-hop, folk and street art, and is often injected with a light-hearted humour. He's also very versatile: working largely in paint, photography and drawing, but also adept in collage, murals, illustrations and zines. A central figure in Norwich's thriving creative scene, Liam also exhibits internationally and was recently selected as a Bloomberg New Contemporaries Artist 2019. • *ew*

SAM HARRONS moved to Norwich in 2009 to study at NUA, and since then has enhanced the creative culture within the city through his various projects. A constant ideas generator with an entrepreneurial streak, Sam finds joy in bringing creative ventures and people together – from the conception of SHHHH Collective through to the wildly successful Tropico events. He co-founded the original Artel café, runs his own design practice, Samu Studio, and has most recently set up GOOOD, an ethical brand directory that connects people with companies who care. His most popular and recognised project to-date is currently in your hands – the SHHHH Guide to Norwich.

Contact
IG @liamashleyclark

Contact
IG @samharrons
samharrons@me.com

HAH Online

Iga Szymanska

HAH ONLINE offers clothing, childrenswear, accessories and homeware that are bright, bold and full of joy – with the bonus of being responsibly-made. Working with small, local businesses and crafters, HAH highlights handmade design, with limited edition pieces and colourful collections that pack a punch. With fully recyclable packaging, HAH is good for the community and the planet. That's why all their products – including their much-loved positivi-tees – raise a smile, with style that is built to last. • *gr*

IGA Szymanska is a textile artist and recent graduate from NUA, where she specialised in printmaking and illustration. An avid sketcher, Iga is rarely seen without a sketchbook and a few colourful markers. Her work – both conceptual and commercial – is inspired by architecture and human nature.

Iga's work is available through her eponymous brand Ignis Szy Art. Her unique products are all ethically made in Britain and can be found in The Giggly Goat and the gift shop at Norwich Castle Museum. • *as*

Contact
hahonline.co.uk
IG @hahonline

Contact
ignisszy.com/shop
IG @ignisszy.art

StudioDo

Location

-

Unit 10, Anderson Yard
NR2 3EL

Contact

-

studiodo.co.uk
infostudiodo@gmail.com

THE ART of ceramics is both a timeless tradition and a highly-fashionable craft. If you've ever thought about making something yourself then you're in luck – StudioDo provides a friendly and nurturing space for beginner potters and ceramic enthusiasts alike to meet and create. We'd recommend signing up to one of their affordable classes or workshops. StudioDo also provides memberships for ceramic artists developing their practice.

StudioDo is a great place to meet like-minded creators who are happy to chat to you about your projects. Sign-up to their newsletter on the website for regular information about classes and studio news. • *jr*

Yora Studio

Emma Lee Cracknell

SISTERS Yly and Alia Tolentino set up their online vintage store, Yora Studio, five years ago with the purpose of decluttering old clothes. It has since blossomed into a carefully curated virtual collection of timeless, comfortable and wearable classic pieces.

Yora's online store stands more as a lookbook. A keen eye for design is apparent; from the quality of garments presented to the way they are thoughtfully styled and injected with fresh direction. Conscious, slow shopping of structured, minimal and quality pieces – that's the Yora way. • *ew*

EMMA LEE CRACKNELL is an emerging abstract artist, educated and working in Norwich. Since graduating from NUA in 2014, Emma has been developing a striking signature style. Her work is rooted in representing emotion that cannot be verbalised; she repurposes the medium to act as voice to communicate the unknown. Her poignant large-scale pieces have caught the attention of national publications, been awarded prestigious awards and showcased in pivotal galleries in Norwich, London and abroad. • *ew*

Contact
yorastudio.com
IG @yora.studio

Contact
emmaleecracknell.co.uk
IG @emmaleecracknellart

Boiler House Press

Location

-

Office MUS1.02,
Inderdisciplinary Institute
for the Humanities
University of East Anglia
Norwich Research Park
NR4 7TJ

Contact

-

boilerhouse.press
IG @boilerhousepress

NORWICH is piled high with independent bookshops and publishers, and one of the most exciting names to emerge in recent years is Boiler House Press.

Based at the University of East Anglia – home to the world-renowned Creative Writing MA – within England's first UNESCO City of Literature, Boiler House is passionate about innovative, mould-breaking literature that plays with (and between) the creative and the critical. Spanning fiction, non-fiction, poetry and everything in-between, their stories are nestled within beautifully-designed, high-quality pages that offer a feast for the eyes as well as the mind.

Check out *Wretched Strangers*, an anthology to mark the vital contribution of non-UK-born writers to the country's literary culture, and their exquisitely put-together poetry and fiction sets. • *sm*

Strangers Press

Location

-

Office MUS 1.02
Interdisciplinary Institute
for the Humanities
University of East Anglia
NR4 7TJ

Contact

-

strangers.press
IG @strangerspress

LOOKING for beautifully presented and wonderfully affecting stories from around the world? Check out Strangers Press, a team dedicated to publishing the finest literature in translation in collaboration with the British Centre for Literary Translation, UEA and the National Centre for Writing.

Borrowing their name from the 16th-century 'Strangers' – a group of migrants fleeing from persecution in their own land, who found themselves welcomed in our city – Strangers Press provide a platform for talented international writers to find new readers in the English language. Projects so far include the KESHIKI Japanese chapbook series, a collaboration with local designers Nigel Aono-Bilson and Glen Robinson, and similarly YEOYU, translated from Korean. Purchase locally from The Book Hive, their website, or from all good bookshops nationwide. • *sm*

little lifts

littlelifts

Contact

-

littlelifts.org.uk
IG @littlelifts_uk

LITTLELIFTS is an inspiring charity helping women with breast cancer. They create 'littlelifts boxes' filled with products aiming to help alleviate some of the side effects that may be experienced during chemotherapy. By donating a small amount of money, you can provide one of these boxes to help women going through what can often be a difficult time. The boxes include goodies such as herbal teas, body lotions, sweets, notebooks, crosswords and hot chocolate – little gestures that make a big difference. • *jr*

Grapes Hill Community Garden

Location

-

7 Swansea Rd
NR2 3HU

Contact

-

07729 540482
grapeshillcommunitygarden.org

THE Grapes Hill Community Garden is a real slice of urban utopia. The small, tranquil green space was converted from a disused former play area between 2008 and 2011 and has been open to the public ever since. Dedicated staff and volunteers grow organic plants, herbs, fruits, and vegetables, which are available for the public to help themselves. The space also hosts a variety of gardening events, workshops, picnics and other meetings. Raised beds are available for private renting, so make sure you don't pick produce from those! • *jc*

Bullards Gin

Location
-
74 - 78 St Benedicts St
NR2 4AR

Contact
-
01603 920292
bullardsspirits.co.uk

ESTABLISHED in 1837, the Bullards name is closely linked with the brewing history of Norwich, and you can still find lots of old Bullards memorabilia in pubs up and down the county. In 2015 the brand was resurrected to focus on the handcrafted production of gin. Their purpose-built distillery is the only distillery in Norwich and the first for over 150 years.

Want to see where the magic happens? Book onto a tour of the distillery to learn about the dark history of gin and the Bullards heritage. Of course, the best bit is getting involved in a gin tasting masterclass with one of their brand ambassadors!

Hemp on Toast

Printer Johnson

HEMP ON TOAST proves that ethically-sourced, environmentally-friendly fashion is comfy, stylish and easily available to you. Born from a desire to bring hemp and its incredible antibacterial, durable and UV-protective qualities to more people, they also promote the concept of a wardrobe that is smaller but full of things that you wear and love regularly. Plus, all of their colours come straight from a natural plant source! Ditch the cotton, and try Hemp on Toast. • *sm*

PRINTER JOHNSON is a paper goods brand and trading name of illustrator and print maker Vicki Johnson. Inspired by nature, folklore and pattern, Vicki designs colourful illustrations with a nostalgic feel from her studio in Norwich. Her collections of high-quality greetings cards, postcard sets and prints are available to buy from her online shop and at wholesale.

Vicki has been part of Norwich's thriving print scene for over 10 years, taking part in print fairs, pop up events and makers' markets locally and nationally.

Contact
hempontoast.co.uk
IG @hempontoast

Contact
printerjohnson.com
IG @printerjohnson

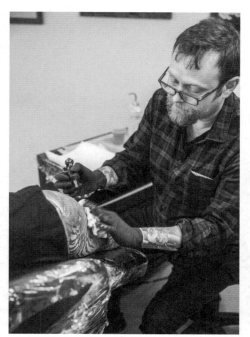

Black Dog Tattoos

Tom Abbiss Smith Art

BLACK DOG is a custom tattoo studio made up of approachable, knowledgeable artists who are passionate about what they do. The studio houses four resident artists – Jon Longstaff, Enzo Barbareschi, Owen Meredith and Helen Riley – as well as a calendar of guest artists hailing from all over; providing original artwork and expert advice that suits each individual. The shop style has its roots in classic Japanese and western traditional tattooing, but also embraces solid black work and fine illustrative styles. • *sm*

TAKING inspiration from the people and things around him, Tom Abbiss Smith creates bold, abstract designs for homeware products, clothing, packaging and much more. Tom works in a variety of mediums, including digital collage, printmaking and painting to produce works for diverse clients such as Made.com, Häagen-Dazs, Bandcamp and Liberty of London. A large part of Tom's creative output stems from Paper Plant Studio, his Norwich-based design brand. • *fs*

Location
47 St Benedicts St
NR2 4PG

Contact
01603 291049
IG @blackdogtattoos

Contact
hello@tomabbisssmithart.com
IG @tomabbisssmithart

Redwell Brewery Co.

Location

-

7 The Arches, Bracondale
NR1 2EF

Contact

-

01603 974288
IG @redwellbrewing

VISITING the Redwell Brewery is a must in Norwich. Whether it's in the warmer months, when you can sit back and enjoy the amazing beer garden, or in winter when you can wrap up cosy with the tanks inside the brewery, you can always be sure of a great community space. Just a couple of minutes' walk from the Football Stadium, Redwell is the perfect place for a pre-match drink, and is welcoming of families and dogs.

Suitable for all beer lovers, Redwell are also experts in vegan and gluten-free craft beers, and often hold pop-up food and social events. • *jr*

Flomotion

The Voice Project

FELLOW desk dwellers, rejoice: Flomotion are revolutionising our workplace wellbeing and helping businesses to embrace active working! Collaborating with organisations and individuals, the team offer office furniture solutions that help workers to improve their posture, feel energised and be more productive. Specialising in sit-stand desks and ergonomic seating, Flomotion champion movement which reduces the back problems and health issues that sedentary working causes, in order to create an environment where workers can excel. • *as*

Location
Capitol House, 4 - 6 Heigham St
NR2 4TE

Contact
flomotionstudio.com
IG @flomotion_studio

THE Voice Project is an open-access community choir with lots of opportunities for you to get involved with inspiring, inclusive and original new music performances. Founded in 2008, it has since involved hundreds of singers in large-scale performances for Norfolk & Norwich Festival, Brighton Festival, London Jazz Festival and others, as well as running useful practical workshops. Whatever your previous experience, if you love to sing, The Voice Project would love to sing with you! • *jr*

Location
90 Upper St Giles St
NR2 1LT

Contact
voiceproject.co.uk
IG @voiceprojectnorwich

Grain Brewery

Location

-

South Farm, Tunbeck Rd
Alburgh, Harleston
IP20 0BS

Contact

-

01986 788884
grainbrewery.co.uk

NORFOLK is world famous for its brewers' barley, and the soul of any great tasting beer is the grain. From their base in Alburgh, Grain Brewery has created a new tradition with its modern bitters and ales, as well as lagered keg beers, wheat beers and a smoked porter. If you fancy seeing how their drinks are made, we recommend going along to one of their open days on the last Saturday of each month. Or if you'd prefer to sample closer to home, you'll find their range at The Cottage on Silver Rd and The Plough on St Benedicts St. • *sm*

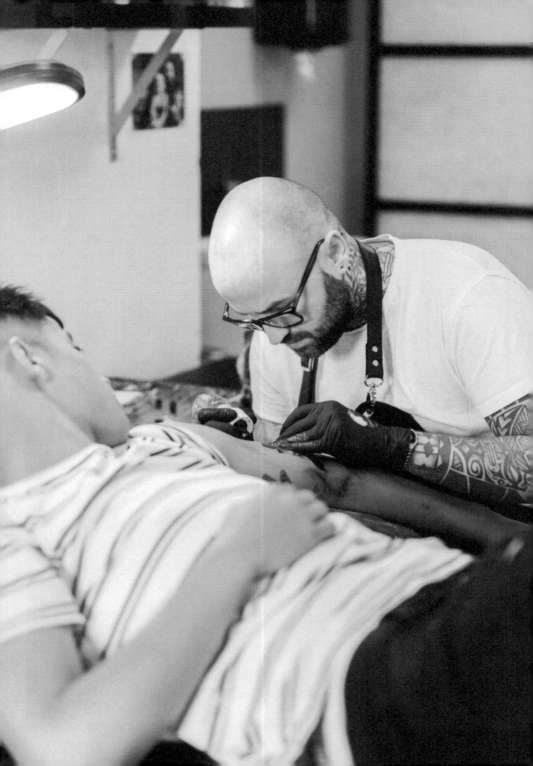

Indigo

Location

-

2 Lower Goat Ln
NR2 1EL

Contact

-

01603 886143
IG @indigotattoostudio

INDIGO Tattoo and Piercing is one of the most established and well-respected studios in Norwich. Specialising in quality custom tattooing since 2004 and disciplined in a range of styles, Indigo has a talented roster of in-house artists as well as regular guests from the UK and beyond. Whatever design you have in mind, the friendly and talented team have got you covered; from mandala and dotwork to black traditional or colour realism. Indigo is also a trusted provider of laser tattoo removal, with laser technician Perry offering free consultations and a test patch on designs you want to cover-up or remove completely.

The shop also offers professional body piercing on a walk-in basis – or if you're feeling brave, intimates by appointment. They use a wide selection of surgical-grade titanium body jewellery and offer free jewellery changes for any healed piercing. Highly recommended for their approachability and experience. • *sm*

services:

Creative Giant

Location
-
28 - 32 St Andrews St
NR2 4AE

Contact
-
07515 397261
creativegiant.co.uk

IF you're looking for a well-established, reputable and talented design agency, then look no further than Rob Wilkes and Creative Giant. You'll find their portfolio across the city with many of Norwich's best independents; from Jive Kitchen to Abode Letting Agents, and Union Building to Grain Brewery. Plus, they were the masterminds behind the attention-grabbing social media campaign 'Anglia Square not Leicester Square' for *Alan Partridge: Alpha Papa!*

Champions of the underdog and passionate supporters of ambitious entrepreneurs, Creative Giant loves working with startups, small businesses and emerging brands, helping them make their mark with a competitive edge. Whether it's developing a brand strategy in a 'Giant Thinking' discovery workshop, crafting a visual identity from scratch or turning the volume up on what you already have, Creative Giant offers a fresh perspective with compelling creative for any sector. • *sm*

Spindle

Location

-

17 Palace St
NR3 1RT

Contact

-

01603 338303
spindle.co

SPINDLE is a production studio that prides itself on developing bold and innovative films – both for entertainment and advertisement. Their work for some of the world's biggest brands (Mercedes-Benz, Nike, Huawei, BT Sport, and the Royal Navy) has been widely praised, landing them multiple awards, including Cannes Lions, British Arrows and Vimeo Staff Picks.

Beyond advertising, Spindle also creates content for the entertainment space. With a diverse roster of award-winning directors, the studio is experienced in making unapologetically modern films that have a profound impact on the viewer. Spindle takes a hands-on approach throughout the creative process – from conception to development, production and beyond – to deliver a result that matches their singular vision. • *fs*

Voewood

Location

-

Cromer Rd
High Kelling
NR25 6QS

Contact

-

01263 713802
voewood.com

HIDDEN in the woods near the wild North Norfolk coast, you'll find an arts and crafts home with a rock & roll heart.

With 17 amazing bedrooms sleeping 41 guests and space for over 150 guests during the day and evening, Voewood is the perfect wedding location as well as an inspired house for celebrating, gathering, partying, retreating, dancing, photographing, product launching or just unwinding and nourishing the soul.

Prime Finish

Location

-

14 Furze Rd
NR7 0AS

Contact

-

07914 495601
primefinishdecorators.co.uk

PRIME Finish Decorators have delivered the highest quality building, renovation and decorating services in Norwich and beyond for over 23 years. They're the biggest perfectionists in the business! Ian and his team have an impressive portfolio – everything from multi-million-pound penthouse apartments to chic office spaces – and employ an experienced staff of tradespeople including carpenters, electricians and bricklayers. They are also well-versed in all forms of interior and exterior painting, wallpapering, commercial decorating, interior design advice and refurbishments/renovations.

Whether you're extending your home, revamping your kitchen or in need of a thoughtfully designed and decorated space to work, make a call to Prime Finish Decorators. • *sm*

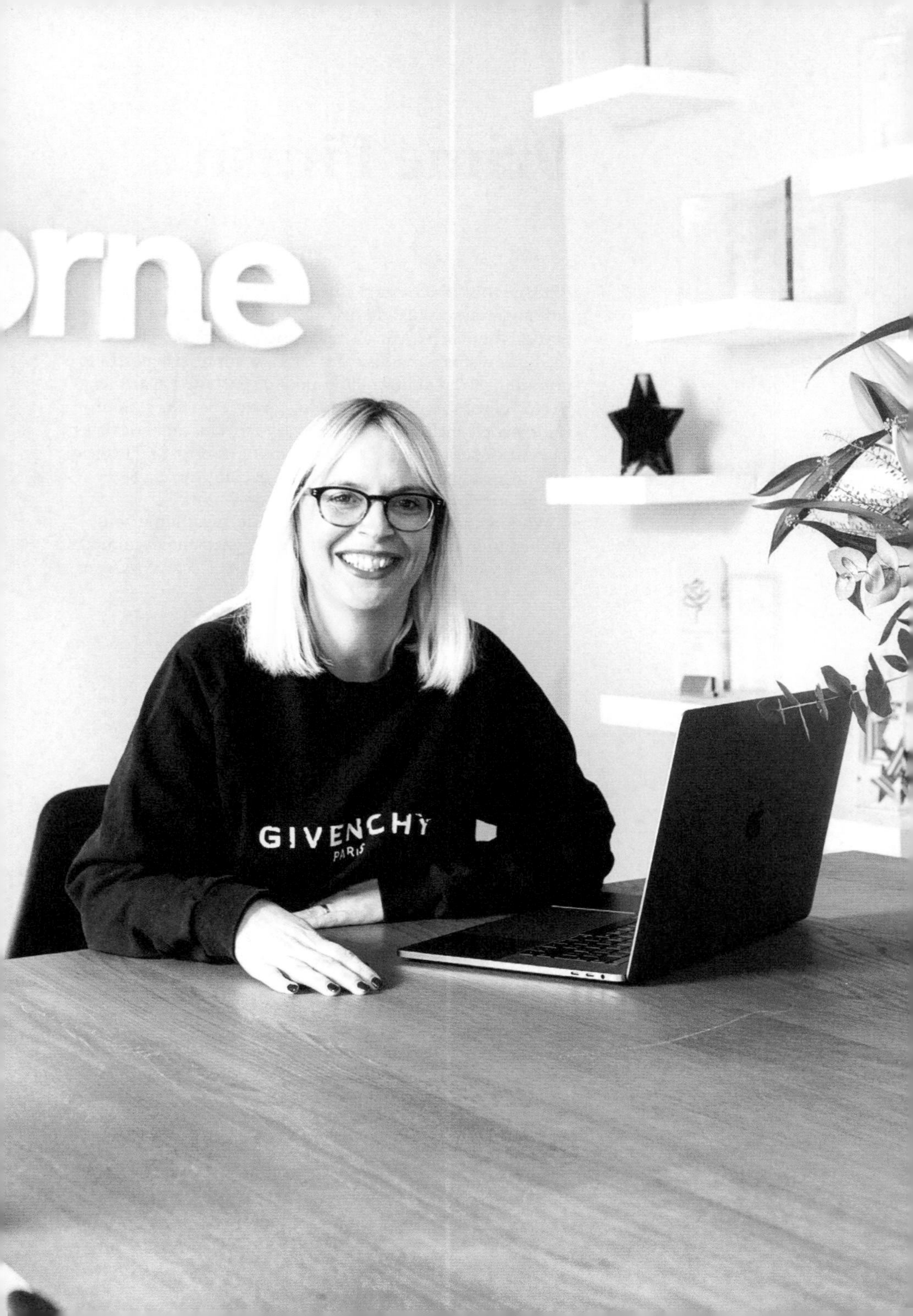
GIVENCHY
PARIS

borne

Contact
-
IG @we_are_borne
weareborne.com

BORNE is an independent creative agency offering businesses creative, strategic, digital and social brilliance. Their multi-award-winning branding, campaigns and websites are founded on a culture of collaboration and an approach bespoke to each client. Offering everything from brand strategy to web development, borne also have a full digital production setup in house. The team work with a diverse range of organisations all over the country and across an array of sectors, creating long-term partnerships with their impressive list of clients that includes UEA, Médecins Sans Frontières and CITB.

At the heart of borne's success is their impressive team; each individual provides a unique set of skills and personality that contributes to ensuring that every project is world-class. The borne family are also key members of the local arts community, frequently taking part in educational and enriching events to develop their skills, as well as supporting colleagues with exciting personal creative projects. • *as*

Lukey's VegBox

Contact
-
07449 957391
lukeysgroceries.com

A LOCAL fave and known to most for their fruit and veg tenure at the Norwich Food Store on St Benedicts, Lukey's Vegbox sprung from a desire to connect fine city locals more closely with their food. A door-to-door grocery delivery service with a keen emphasis on fresh, locally-sourced produce with minimal eco packaging, they pride themselves on their one-to-one relationship with customers. Perfect for those wanting to reconnect with how their food is sourced. • *sh*

The Click

Contact
-
01603 626249
theclickdesign.com

THE Click is a brand-led design studio – creating identities with ideas. They are widely regarded as the 'go-to' agency for the creation or reinvention of brand identities.

Led by creative director, Bobby Burrage, The Click create bold, recognisable and engaging brands for independent artisans to global enterprises. From artificial intelligence to antique dealers, from breweries to bakeries, from cathedrals to chocolatiers.

Working with businesses both established and new, The Click pinpoint what makes each organisation unique and express it in a simple, truly memorable way. Their ideas-based design champions moments, insights and connections; combining a clean, contemporary graphic style with a real knack for knowing what makes people tick. • *as*

Hudson Architects

Location

-

37 St Andrews St
NR2 4TP

Contact

-

01603 766220
hudsonarchitects.co.uk

HAVING featured twice on *Grand Designs*, including the prestigious RIBA House of the Year, we're proud to have one of the UK's leading design-led architecture practices on our doorstep. Hudson Architects boasts a stunning portfolio of award-winning buildings ranging from bespoke homes to boutique hotels, art galleries and museums. They are the team behind Norwich's best-loved cultural buildings including OPEN, NUA's Boardman House and East Gallery, and they're an active and trusted voice in cultural place-making across the region.

With an ethos of sustainability at their core, the practice produces low energy, healthy buildings without compromising on high-end design. Be it an arts venue, classroom or a private family home, Hudson Architects create beautiful, inspiring spaces for people to inhabit.

Blackstar Dog Training

Contact
-
07747 015678
blackstardogs.com

YOUR dog is unique and so is your relationship to one another: that's why Blackstar Dog Training offers individually tailored sessions in and around Norwich, providing you with the skills needed to nurture the perfect bond with your dog. Founder Tim James uses enjoyable, modern training techniques entirely based on kind-to-the-dog positivity. Tim is an expert in understanding why things are 'going wrong' and will teach you to how to create a dialogue and work as a team with your dog; showing you how to communicate effectively, as well as gently guiding them in the right direction for outstanding results. • *jr*

Make It Move

Location

-

St George's Works
51 Colegate
NR3 1DD

Contact

-

01603 905980
makeitmove.co.uk

NORFOLK-BORN and NUA-educated, Stephen and Mark run 'Make It Move', a Norwich-based animation studio which works towards bringing stories to life. The duo have over eight years of experience together, producing TV, apps, games and social media animation for a roster of impressive clients. They've delivered recognisable branding for a number of companies both around the world and closer to home here in Norwich. Offering creative direction, animation and sound design, the team are as adept at delivering projects at global film festivals as they are at 'the World's smallest Cinema' at Glastonbury. You can certainly trust the pair to bring whatever your story may be to life! • *ew*

Page Bros

Location

-

Mile Cross Ln
NR6 6SA

Contact

-

01603 778800
pagebros.co.uk

WONDER how we managed to make such a beautiful piece of print? Look no further than Page Bros, a supplier of quality print services for more than 260 years in Norwich.

Originating in 1746 as a family-owned brush manufacturers before evolving into printing, Page Bros remain a fully independent company that can be counted on for all of your business communication needs. Typesetting, Litho Printing and Binding, Digital Print and Finishing, Security Printing, even Storage and Distribution. It's all there.

Delivered by a skilled and talented team with a level of quality and attention to detail of the highest order, Page Bros will turn your ideas into reality. With regular clients including UEA, NUA and our very own *SHHH Guide*, we couldn't recommend them more highly.

They print. They create. They fulfil. They enable. Enough said.

St. George's Works

Location

-

51 Colegate
NR3 1DD

Contact

-

01603 219753
stgeorgesworks.uk

A PIECE of history re-invented as an integral space in Norwich's present; St. George's Works is a flexible, affordable and inspiring workspace.

Originally a factory, the space now nurtures productivity by offering a range of working spaces fit for any business venture. With meeting rooms, a boardroom, rooftop terrace (with great views of the city!), private offices and entire floors available, St George's Works offers large, open spaces designed to echo their creative location: being close to Norwich's thriving and creative Lanes.

Other benefits to the space include flexible terms, on-site support and links with their sister site in Spitalfields, making it ideal for professionals with contacts in London. • *ew*

Gracie's Dog Walking Service

Location
-

Norwich areas covered:
NR1, NR2 and NR4

Contact
-

07557 273724
graciesdogwalkingservice.co.uk

NEED a dog walker? Loyal and trustworthy, Gracie's Dog Walking Service offers a range of services including group and solo dog walks, daily pop-in puppy visits and cat visits while you're away on holiday. Grace always strives to give her clients the best possible experience, offering free consultations with no obligation to use her services afterwards. Plus, the van that Grace uses to transport the pets that she's looking after is fully kitted out with high-quality cages. • *fs*

The Fire Pit Camp

Location

-

The Firs, Nr Dereham Rd
Wendling, NR19 2LT

Contact

-

thefirepitcamp.co.uk
Sarah: 07917 406953
Rachel: 07717 315 199

AMIDST the rustling breeze of the Norfolk countryside lies the family-run private campsite, The Fire Pit Camp. Situated not too far from Dereham and Swaffham, the campsite is easily accessible to the North Norfolk coast and Norwich and boasts the natural beauty of the surrounding area.

Available to hire for events such as festivals, weddings, ceremonies and fully equipped for glamping, The Fire Pit Camp has a licensed warehouse bar and an on-site hazel bender tent. As stunning as it is versatile, the site has also played host to the ever popular 'Most Curious Wedding Fair', which showcases homegrown wedding suppliers throughout Norfolk. Also on site sits the Yoga Yurt, a peaceful embrace of the quiet surroundings, where Sarah, partner and founder of the campsite, runs regular yoga sessions.

Boasting the natural elegance of the country landscape, The Fire Pit Camp is a natural choice for all occasions. • *sh*

Lighting Technologies

DECK

FUNCTIONAL design and detail drives the core mechanism of Lighting Technologies. A business tucked on the intersection of Lower Goat Lane and St Andrews, all manner of lighting needs are managed expertly. From architectural ambient lighting for environments such as hotels and home decor to smaller lamp needs, Lighting Technologies not only supply but also project design and installation. Illuminated by 30 years of experience, every detail is considered to ensure the right fit. • *sh*

Location
St George's Works, 51 Colegate
NR3 1DD

Contact
lightingtechnologies.co.uk
steven@lightingtechnologies.co.uk

DECK produces eye-catching, bespoke balloon installations for all sorts of places and occasions, including dance floors, shop windows and bars.

Beyond their look and function, DECK define themselves by their environmentally-conscious approach to what they do. All the balloons they use are totally biodegradable and they choose not to fill them with helium.

Too often, we're made to experience art as divorced from fun, and vice versa. This certainly isn't the case with DECK, who's installations are both thought-provoking and fun. • *fs*

Contact
info@deckitout.co.uk
IG @deck_above

NILE

ESP Merchandise

TEACHERS from all over the world are drawn to Norwich Institute for Language Education (NILE) every year for the UK's highest-rated short professional development courses for language teachers. As well as academic excellence including the CELTA (the Cambridge-awarded initial TEFL qualification), NILE has offered homestay accommodation, cultural programmes, school visits and business placements, encouraging international interaction in the local community since 1995. • *gr*

SPECIALISING in garment screen printing and embroidery, ESP Merchandise has an environmentally-friendly approach, with little environmental impact.

Having provided services to a number of prestigious brands and independent businesses, ESP Merchandise are ideal for any specialist or bespoke needs. Ethical, professional and efficient, this is one of the best places for screen printing in Norwich: be it hoodies, caps, polo shirts, tees or tote bags. • *ec*

Location
78 - 80 Upper St Giles St
NR2 1LT

Contact
01603 664473
nile-elt.com

Location
5 Spar Rd
NR6 6BY

Contact
01603 484000
espmerchandise.com

Quanström Studio

Location

-

136 Magdalen St
NR3 1JD

Contact

-

01603 440601
quanstromstudio.com

TAKE a walk to the north end of Magdalen St and you'll find Quanström Studio – a handsome, welcoming store and wood workshop selling clean, minimal furniture, customisable to your needs and made on site with local materials.

Alive with music and the hum of creativity, the studio is run by craftsman, designer and owner Dan Quanström, alongside partner-in-craft Chanti Clark and their Irish terrier Captain. Dan's handmade work features alongside carefully selected artisanal items from friends across the UK, and a tasty selection of limited-edition records from Venus Vinyl.

Testament to their clear passion for the work, Dan and Chanti are equally capable of creating a bespoke piece to set off your living room, or undertaking a full design and build for your project. Head to Quanström Studio for a chat about your exciting ideas or find them in one of the great local pubs surrounding the area.

GrafikLanguage

Location

-

5 Rigby's Court
NR2 1NT

Contact

-

07833 153810
grafiklanguage.agency

GRAFIKLANGUAGE is an agency specialising in words: copywriting, branding, naming, scriptwriting, training, and strategy. Crafting clear, compelling copy is at the heart of what they do.

They work with some of the region's most respected brands, organisations, and agencies including Hoseasons, UEA, NUA, Original Cottages, Redwell Brewing, Woodforde's, and Norfolk County Council. Plus they're creative partners with Norwich BID and VisitNorwich to rebrand the city, developing a new narrative for the City of Stories. Further afield, their clients include Proskauer in New York, Eastpak in Belgium, and Beyond agency in San Francisco.

Co-founded three years ago by Kelly and Charlie, best friends who met at the University of Cambridge, the agency's grown into a core team of seven. Kelly, Tammer, and Daisy are all proud MA Creative Writing alumni from the University of East Anglia.

Ark

Location

-

25 St John Maddermarket
NR2 1DN

Contact

-

01603 465335
designbyark.co.uk

ARK is a design studio, co-founded by award-winning creatives, Simon McWhinnie, Lee Nash and Neil Wright. Based in the heart of the Norwich Lanes, they help small and large businesses to grow and evolve through ideas-led brand communications.

Recently, Ark became a creative partner with VisitNorwich and Norwich BID, working on the exciting city rebrand. Other clients include Jarrold, Norwich University of the Arts, Liftshare, and Norwich City Football Club.

With an ever-increasing portfolio of brands, and a growing reputation for impactful, memorable work, Ark is continuing to build on its ambition to become a leading design studio in the East.

Eye Film

Location

-

112 -114 Magdalen St
Norwich NR3 1JD

Contact

-

eyefilm.co.uk
@eye__film

EYE FILM are an award winning production company who have been a driving force in the East Anglian Film scene for nearly 50 years. Nestled in Norwich's true creative heartland of Magdalen St, they produce documentaries, features and promotional content with businesses, broadcasters and charities from around the world.

Storytelling is always in focus and their roots in documentary filmmaking run through everything they do, specialising in drawing out the details and making beautiful, thought-provoking work. As a team of creatives – from artists and photographers to DJs, writers and designers – they make creativity their objective and the driving force behind all the work they produce.

pubs and bars:

Norwich Playhouse

Location
-
42 - 58 St Georges St
NR3 1AB

Contact
-
IG @norwichplayhouse
norwichplayhouse.co.uk

ONE of the most iconic venues in Norwich, the Playhouse Bar is known for its amazing atmosphere and brilliant creative cardboard ceiling city. With a beautiful riverside terrace, bright-coloured benches, and ever-changing artwork, it's a firm favourite for students and creative types in particular. There's a great selection of local ales and more exotic drinks to choose from, as well as teas, coffees, hot chocolate and juices to suit every occasion. You'll also find a rotating schedule of art exhibitions from local artists and music played both live and on vinyl. Great for a casual catch-up with friends or for a pre-show drink before heading into the Playhouse auditorium (*p195*).

Bermuda Bob's Rum Shack

Location

-

7A Timber Hill
NR1 3JZ

Contact

-

IG @bermudabobs

ATOP Timberhill, amongst barbers, bakeries and bespoke clothing boutiques, lies a tropical venture dedicated to the rising craft of rum. Bermuda Bob's Rum Shack omits the same quirky atmosphere as it's sister bar, Gonzo's Tea Room; crafting a booze-cruise ambience amidst shelves laden with rum, tiki tropical decor and jungle spruces.

Boasting an impressive menu of 170 rums, Bermuda Bob's craft balmy cocktails befit for a beach getaway. Once the second dwelling of Norwich's DIY punk pub The Owl Sanctuary, Bob's now embraces a varied diary of DJ nights dedicated to jazz, funk, soul and disco – with a few comedy nights thrown in for good measure. Decked in swathes of beach shack souvenirs, the bar caters for those looking to dance as well as social meet ups in the downstairs bar booths. Concocting thematic fun with serious rum expertise, this hidden gem is a must visit. • *sh*

Gonzo's Tea Room

Location

-

68 London St
NR2 1JT

Contact

-

01603 473763
gonzostearoom.com

NOTORIOUS as it is iconic, Gonzo's defies easy interpretation. Hustling as a chic coffee hangout and boasting the best burgers in town during the day, by sundown the Tea Rooms become an electric hubbub of nightlife entertainment. Whether they play host to live comedy, intimate drag nights or sharp DJ sets, you best believe they do it with a motley menu of cocktails served with homespun swagger. Named after the owner's adorable pet pug, Gonzo, the bar is swathed in novelty relics and trinkets which add to the offbeat spirit, as soft furnishings invite you in for a cozy evening.

Gonzo's caters for all occasions. Whether you're seeking a casual date night or an eclectic open mic, they curate only the best events with a private terrace also available to hire. Found in the heart of the city's nightlife, Gonzo's is one not to be missed. • *sh*

Bar Tapas

Location

-

16-20 Exchange St
NR2 1AT

Contact

-

01603 764077

CELEBRATING the philosophy and spirit of Spain and South America, Bar Tapas is a colourfully-decorated restaurant serving delicious tapas dishes and drinks. But it's so much more than that! It was one of the first rays of hope in Norwich nightlife: for those who don't want to go home when the pubs shut but can't bear to face the Prince of Wales crowd, this humble restaurant, hidden in plain sight above a shop on Exchange St, might as well be Studio 54. Tables shoved aside, rumba and salsa blaring, Spanish beer and snacks on the bar is exactly how life should be. Highly recommended. • *jc*

Frank's Bar

Location

-

19 Bedford St
NR2 1AR

Contact

-

01603 618902
franksbar.co.uk

FRANK'S BAR is effortlessly cool but still relaxed, welcoming and free of pretension. During the day it's a chilled location for a coffee and a slice of cake with friends; but come evening, their extensive drinks menu really comes into its own. Add to that their delicious Mediterranean and North African-inspired food – including veggie and vegan dishes and an excellent daily breakfast menu running Tue - Sat until noon and 10am - 6pm on Sunday – plus regular live music and film screenings, and Frank's truly becomes a bar for all occasions. • *tmu*

The Bowling House

Location

-

7 Dereham Rd
NR2 4HX

Contact

-

01603 397412
IG @thebowlinghouse

THE BOWLING HOUSE is an excellent way to spend an evening or leisurely afternoon. Mixing great food and delicious drinks with five intimate bowling lanes, the alley, restaurant and bar offers a good time for everyone.

Each lane has an exceptionally maintained dark wood pin-deck which, alongside the contemporary interior, low lighting and quirky art, ensure a fun, retro atmosphere. With bumpers, ramps and lighter balls available (and even karaoke for those who don't fancy a bowl!) The Bowling House caters for families, couples and groups in equal measure. Bowling is priced per person, per game and students, teachers, retired folk and NHS workers get an extra 10% off.

Diners visiting the restaurant will be bowled over by the choice of flavoursome dishes, including tapas, burgers and plenty of veggie options, served alongside a great selection of beers, wines and cocktails. Go on – eat, drink and bowl! • *as*

The Birdcage

Location

-

23 Pottergate

NR2 1DS

Contact

-

01603 633534

thebirdcagenorwich.co.uk

THE BIRDCAGE, in the hub of the Norwich Lanes, is a mainstay in the city's burgeoning art scene and is renowned for it's programming of unique events. From disco to drag, pop-ups to life drawing and cabaret to comedy, it has become a much-loved venue for hosting local and national acts in their intimate downstairs space. Redesigned in the Art Deco style in the 1930s to mimic the façade of a steamliner, it became the Birdcage in 2006 when the current team stepped aboard. With a huge selection of spirits, beers and cocktails, plus the fact you can bring your chips in from Grosvenor Fish Bar opposite, it truly does stand out as a pub in a million.

The Sir Garnet

Location

-

36 Market Pl
NR2 1RD

Contact

-

01603 615892
thesirgarnet.co.uk

WITH City Hall, the buzzing Market and the lavish Royal Arcade all nearby, this intimate dog-friendly pub is a much-loved favourite of locals and sightseers alike and is an ideal place to pitstop after exploring the city. Steeped in history throughout, the building (which dates back to Medieval times) features a room dedicated to the work of the photographer George Plunkett who archived the changing face of Norwich throughout the last century. Offering delicious snacks, classic pub dishes, a great Sunday roast and local ales, it's no surprise that 'everything's all Sir Garnet' means 'all is right'. • *gr*

The Wallow

Location

-

36 Exchange St
NR2 1AX

Contact

-

01603 446676
wallowwine.co.uk

THE WALLOW is a unique bar with an ever-changing selection of wine on tap. Using unique self-service wine dispensing machines, customers can choose from over 50 different white, red, rosé and sparkling wines which can be purchased by inserting a prepaid card. The Wallow presents three whole floors of wine to explore and small samples are available for each offering, so the wine can be tried before committing to a larger glass. Vegan and organic wines are also included in the selection, and the innovative dispensing cabinets mean each drink is kept at the optimal temperature.

Perfect for after work drinks, dates and long, lazy evenings with friends, The Wallow also offers delicious Mediterranean-style cheese and charcuterie platters, as well as tapas dishes to complement their wine menu. Sip your selection by the open fire on a Saturday afternoon and enjoy the relaxed, informal atmosphere, or visit on Wine Wednesdays, when you'll get 25% off all wine between 5pm - 9pm. • *as*

Gin Temple

Location

-

6 Pottergate
NR2 1DS

Contact

-

01603 944079
gintemple.co.uk

SPRINGING UP in the heart of the Lanes, Gin Temple is an effervescent new bar celebrating all things gin. Boasting an indoor garden amongst the many multi-functional spaces at this locally-grown establishment for gin enthusiasts, punters can even pick fresh herbs to compliment their drink of choice. Accompanying their vast menu of Norfolk brewed gins, Gin Temple offers bespoke tasting sessions to share their robust knowledge of the beverage and even accommodates private party function hire. A spirited bar that is bountifully enthusiastic and knows its business, this is a great pick for those looking to broaden their taste. • *sh*

The Unthank Arms

Location

-

149 Newmarket St
NR2 2DR

Contact

-

01603 631557
theunthankarms.com

THE UNTHANK ARMS is our dream idea of a neighborhood pub. We certainly can't think of a better place to visit on a Sunday afternoon for a roast dinner and a pint of real ale. Classically Victorian in style, the atmosphere is warm and welcoming, the decor is tasteful, the food is delicious and fairly priced, and the drinks are carefully chosen. The Unthank is particularly good for larger parties and celebrations, with an upstairs event space available for hire and a large outdoor area for whiling away the summer afternoons. If it's not your local, make sure you make the trip. • *jc*

The William and Florence

Location
-
111 Unthank Rd
NR2 2PE

Contact
-
01603 660706
williamandflorence.co.uk

CANDIDLY cool, The William and Florence is awash with teal touches and contemporary living interiors. It's less of a restaurant and more a light and airy space to relax with an award-winning beer, enjoy top-notch food and catch up with friends. Open all day, seven days a week, The William and Florence were first to serve a 'Bottomless Brunch' on the weekend in Norwich and are mindful to ensure vegan and vegetarian options are creatively catered for. Owned by the partner duo behind The Unthank Arms and three other pubs across Norwich, The William and Florence perfectly complements the Golden Triangle chic of Unthank Road. • *sh*

Chambers Cocktail Company

Location

-

12 - 14 Wensum St
NR3 1HY

Contact

-

01603 633122
chamberscocktailcompany.co.uk

THERE are people that work as bartenders and there are people that *are* bartenders. Chambers Cocktail Company embodies the latter, serving exceptional quality, unique cocktails made with homemade and local ingredients in a welcoming atmosphere. Just moments away from Tombland in the picturesque Cathedral Quarter, the Chambers team go above and beyond to offer you a bespoke experience where their passion and knowledge for cocktail making shines through; ensuring your drink is made just the way you like it, time and time again. And if you fancy a break between cocktails, there's a wide selection of craft beers, classic and modern spirits and wines too. • *jr*

The Bicycle Shop

Location
-

17 St Benedicts St
NR2 4PE

Contact
-

01603 625777
IG @thebicycleshopnorwich

THE BICYCLE SHOP on St. Benedicts Street remains a go-to favourite for sipping, drinking and dining from morning to night. The name is a reference to the building's 82-year history as a bicycle sales and repair shop, but now they mainly fix broken hearts and hungry tummies. Spread across three eccentrically decorated floors, you'll feel like you're visiting your mad artistic aunt for a cup of tea. Vegetarians and vegans are well looked after on their menu, which offers everything from smaller plates for sharing to larger dishes. A well-priced wine list is overseen by friendly and capable staff, but cocktails and beer are the order of the evening here. A particularly well-researched and keenly priced beer bottle list complements the fresh food from the kitchen, which stays open later than most in the city. Make sure you explore the basement; a great spot for drinking absinthe, eating supper and for hosting private events. • *jc*

Panda

Location

-

8 Redwell St
NR2 4SN

Contact

-

01603 610500
pandanorwich.com

PANDA has quickly made itself at home in the building that once housed the iconic Norwich Taphouse. Offering a fresh take on the classic wine bar, Panda specialises in rare and unique drinks in distinctive and quirky surroundings.

From craft beer to local gin, whisky to port, sherry to cocktails, Panda offers a huge variety of drinks. If you're looking for a specific Italian prosecco or a special Merlot, chances are that they have what you're looking for!

With their city-centre location stretched over two floors, guests can either sit upstairs by a well lit, inviting bar, or downstairs in the historic candlelit crypt. Panda is the perfect spot for every occasion – dates, drinks with friends, hen parties and work catch-ups. • *fs*

The Rumsey Wells

Location
-
4 St Andrews St
NR2 4AF

Contact
-
01603 614858
rumseywells.co.uk

AMBLING a mere walk away from the city centre towards the bar and coffee shop metropolis of St. Benedicts St, The Rumsey Wells serves as the ever faithful stalwart of Fine City ales, rum and a mecca for eclectic nights out. Amidst the hubbub of DJ nights and gigs you will find a cosy bar with stairs that meander downwards into the 'Underbelly', an intimate venue space that plays hosts to local gigs, art exhibitions and private hire. Patronise yourselves into the 'Rum Club' by supping from the impressive rum menu and finish it with a side of Pieminister pie. • *sh*

Pear Tree Inn

Location

-

79 Unthank Rd
NR2 2PE

Contact

-

peartreeinnnorwich.com
IG @peartreeinnnorwich

AN ECLECTIC family-run pub in the heart of Norwich's Golden Triangle, The Pear Tree Inn has a great laid-back atmosphere and is completely child and dog friendly – the ideal place for a chat, dinner and a boogie! Husband-and-wife landlords Nick and Lesley have a wealth of experience and enthusiasm between them, including 20 years' experience running award-winning bars and nightclubs across the world. They've got your pub staples covered, including a great menu, a range of beers on tap and regular live music. In winter, there's a toasty open fire to keep you warm, and in summer you can kick back on the beautiful outdoor decking with a cold beer or jug of Pimms.

After you've partied through the night, come back and carve out a spot in the Morning Room – a pleasant spot for a roast and to soak up that 'Sunday feeling'. The perfect antidote to a sore head! • *jr*

The Mash Tun

Location

-

16 Charing Cross
NR2 4AL

Contact

-

01603 622111
IG @the_mash_tun_

FROM its prime location on Charing Cross and near St Benedicts, The Mash Tun revels in serving craft beers and a cacophony of gin in their self-styled 'Gin Palace'. Oozing decadent but rustic decor, there are several floors to traverse, each one with a differing vibe. Travel upstairs to find the Gin Palace, or stay downstairs for a chilled evening of indie brewed beers. The Mash Tun also plays host to many events, from housing music nights for Norwich's independent punk scene, to a regular board games evening. A comfortable bar, perfect for a chic catch up with friends. • *sh*

The Gin Palace

Location

-

16 Charing Cross
NR2 4AL

Contact

-

01603 622111
IG @theginpalacenorwich

HIDDEN away behind an innocuous staircase in the Mash Tun, the Gin Palace is a paradise for those who love the 'other' English beverage. A far cry from the squalor of Hogarth's famous Gin Lane, The Gin Palace transports you to a 20's style cocktail bar with ambient lighting, cosy leather seating, tidily dressed servers, and, of course, gin. Lots of it. Naturally, the bartenders are competent mixologists so alongside an impressive menu of gins expertly paired with tonics and garnishes, you'll find a cocktail on their list to cure what ails you. Perfect for a friends night out or a romantic evening. • *sm*

The Stanley

Location

-

33 Magdalen Rd
NR3 4LG

Contact

-

IG @thestanleynr3

A STALWART of the Magdalen Street pub crawl, The Stanley has undergone a huge makeover from the owner of The Black Horse. The newly-refurbished pub delights in dulcet dark blue hues offset with plush modern furniture for a glorious comforting contemporary vibe.

Brandishing craft beers, cocktails and rotating real ales, The Stanley also has an inspired menu of small sharing plates of food drawn from all over the world. With regular vegan options such as 'southern fried cauliflower wings and vegan mayo', the pub caters for the modern punter, whilst also ensuring tried and tested favourites such as burgers and modern breakfast fry ups remain on the menu. Open from 9.30am Saturdays and Sundays, their breakfast and brunch are not to be missed; and on Tuesday evenings 'Danger Dave' plays host to The Stanley's jubilant pub quiz. A sheer delight, The Stanley is a fave. • *sh*

The Black Horse

Location

-

50 Earlham Rd
NR2 3DE

Contact

-

theblackhorsenorwich.net
IG @the_black_horse

STANDING stoically at the juncture between Dereham Rd and Earlham Rd and a stone's throw from the city centre, The Black Horse remains ever-fixed in the fabric of Norwich – having traded as a public house since 1714. A bastion to the city's pub heritage, the premises boasts some iconic architecture; with striking black window frames set in the red brick of a bygone era, the building retains its historical roots whilst embracing contemporary white signage. The building is one of few in Norwich which survived the war and this rich history is celebrated in photographs exhibited throughout the pub. Serving real ales and a selection of wines, beers and ciders, The Black Horse also offers a delectable dining experience which includes breakfast, lunch and dinner. The menu varies from small and large plates to true pub classics, and even manages to rustle up excellent choices for vegans. • *sh*

The Trafford Arms

Location
-
61 Grove Rd
NR1 3RL

Contact
-
01603 628466
traffordarms.co.uk

BEER fans, rejoice: The Trafford Arms serve an ever-changing selection of superb cask ales, bottled and canned craft beers. A former Norwich and Norfolk CAMRA Branch Pub of the Year, the pub has also held the Cask Marque since 1997, proof of their cellar team's unwavering commitment to the best possible pint.

Truly a pub for the people, The Trafford Arms is a friendly, community-centric venue that offers something for everyone. On top of the delicious food menu and wine list, visitors can also take their pick from a varied calendar of events including quizzes, wine tastings, themed menu nights and – of course – the annual beer festival. • *as*

The Last Pub Standing

Location

-

27 - 29 King St
NR1 1PD

Contact

-

01603 937013
lastpubstanding.co.uk

WE'VE all heard that Norwich once had a pub for every day of the year – but did you know that there was once 58 pubs on King St alone? Today it's down to just one: fortunately, The Last Pub Standing is here to ensure we can raise a glass to these lost taverns in cosy, quirky style. With an excellent choice of drinks, a delicious all-day menu and exciting events list, this gastropub also offers the 'best roast dinner in the city' on a Sunday. Boasting a spacious garden and rooftop terrace, The Last Pub Standing is the perfect spot to relax, come rain or shine. Cheers to that! • *as*

wellbeing
and active:

The Den

Location

-

18B Lower Goat Ln
NR2 1EL

Contact

-

01603 624523
thedenbarbers.co.uk

NESTLED in the heart of the Norwich Lanes, The Den is an independent barbershop that's a huge hit with locals and students alike. With no appointments necessary, swing by for a gander and you'll soon see why.

The shop speaks for itself. Its unique interior creates a cool, contemporary vibe whilst the laid back atmosphere ensures everyone feels at home. Throw in great pricing (including an excellent student discount) and the understated expertise of the friendly team and it's a no-brainer really.

The boys at The Den have a boatload of experience between them so you can rest assured your barnet is in safe hands. They can knock out the classics in their sleep but it's their ahead of the curve pioneering of the latest trends that really sets them apart. From lads to gentlemen, The Den caters to everyone; ensuring your crowning glory is always at it's best, whatever you're after.

Flint

Location

-

6 Upper Goat Ln
NR2 1EW

Contact

-

IG @flint_hair_
flinthair.co.uk

AS A CITY, Norwich embraces its historical traditions whilst remaining at the forefront of fresh and modern creative industries – and Flint Hair Salon is the perfect encapsulation of this balance.

Having relocated to a beautiful three-storey building in Norwich Lanes, Flint provide a wide range of hair cutting and colouring services, undertaken by an experienced team who embody and perfectly complement the skills and attention to detail that owner Conor has honed during his distinguished two-decade career. An appointment at Flint is a relaxed affair, with staff taking the time to ensure you leave with great hair and some creative inspiration courtesy of the changing art on the walls. • *tmu*

Truman's of Norwich

Location

-

38 Elm Hill
NR3 1HG

Contact

-

trumansofnorwich.co.uk
IG @trumansofnorwich

TRUMAN'S has been making the gentlemen of Norwich look and feel their best for years. Based on the historic Elm Hill, the team offer haircuts, grooming and styling for the modern man in an efficient, friendly space. Founders Jason and Alec each have over 25 years of professional barbering experience, and also count a British Barbers Association 'Hall of Fame' winner amongst their team. Dedicated to delivering the sharpest cuts, fades and beard trims coupled with a healthy dose of banter, the whole Truman's clan take their superior service personally, only using products that they themselves have tried and tested. • *as*

Dynamic Fitness

Location

-

93 Ber St
NR1 3EY

Contact

-

IG @dynamicfitnessnorwich
getdynamic.co.uk

WORKING from their vibrant city-centre space, Dynamic Fitness helps clients to make positive changes and achieve their fitness goals in a light, spacious and well-equipped studio. This team of qualified, professional personal trainers is headed up by founder and experienced trainer Ross Lenton, who first established the studio in 2008.

Whether a client is looking to lose weight, improve body tone, rehabilitate after injuries or simply boost their confidence and keep stress levels in check, Dynamic Fitness can help; with tailored one-to-one training and a range of fitness classes for all ages and fitness levels. • *as*

CourageNoble

Location

-

68a King St
NR1 1PG

51 St Giles St
NR2 1JR

Contact

-

couragenoble.com
IG @couragenobleuk

COURAGENOBLE is a barbershop with a difference. Championing community, creativity and local talent, the team offer more than just haircuts. As well as passion for their craft and dedication to each wash, cut and shave, staff are committed to promoting fellow Norwich independents: their stores are a unique blend of design and creativity, where customers can sip coffee roasted by Strangers or a specialty beer from Redwells below framed work by local artists. They also do their best to help the environment by offering shampoo and conditioner in refillable bottles.

Enjoy outstanding service from an exceptionally friendly, talented team and come away from the King St or St Giles St store with a sharp new look, courtesy of some of Norwich's finest. • *as*

ZenMuma

Contact

-

07813 069529

IG @zenmuma

NEW motherhood can be tricky to navigate. That's why Norwich-born yoga and hypnobirthing teacher training school ZenMuma aims to empower and support pregnant women, birthing couples and mothers along their journey. By training women to become specialised yoga and hypnobirthing teachers, more women can have calmer pregnancies and births, and receive the essential post-natal support they need in yoga classes taught by ZenMuma teachers.

ZenMuma is more than their courses; it is a community. With a range of flexible course options, ZenMuma seeks to support those who share their passions for women, pregnancy, birth and babies and wish to become part of the family.

The Pilates Norwich Studio

Location

-

Labour in Vain Yard
Guildhall Hill
NR2 1JD

Contact

-

07891 987055
thepilatesstudionorwich.com

HIDDEN in a quiet spot in the Norwich Lanes, Labour in Vain Yard is home to The Pilates Studio Norwich. Lauren and her team teach the Classical Pilates repertoire and are passionate about using Pilates to improve your fitness and overall well-being.

The bright and spacious studio is equipped for group and private Apparatus and Mat classes, suitable for all abilities and ages. Whether you're recovering from a sports injury or dealing with back pain from spending too much time at your desk, the combination of controlled stretching and strengthening will work wonders and help you find muscles you didn't know existed!

Hench Herbivore

Capoeira Communities

NUTRITIONIST and former Personal Trainer Paul Kerton is Norwich's very own vegan fitness and nutrition expert! He runs the popular 'Hench Herbivore' YouTube channel, has appeared on TV and radio and was featured in top fitness magazine Muscle & Fitness. He also helped encourage Mr Universe 2014 Barny du Plessis to go vegan, resulting in them becoming training partners. Paul offers personalised nutrition and workout plans via email; if you're looking to improve your fitness and nutrition, make him your first port of call. • sh

LOOKING for a new way to keep fit, build confidence or do something creative and different? Get in touch with Capoeira Communities (Capocoms), an art outreach organisation that aims to spread knowledge of the Afro-Brazilian game of Capoeira through movement, music and language. Delivering workshops in this unique cultural tradition to local schools and communities, Capocoms also runs weekly classes that are suitable for complete beginners in both adults and children. • jr

Location
2 - 3 St Mary's Works
Oak Street, NR3 3AF

Location
Trinity URC Hall, 22 Unthank Rd
NR2 2RA

Contact
henchherbivore@yahoo.co.uk
henchherbivore.com

Contact
coolcapoeira@gmail.com
capocoms.org.uk

Treat

Spruce House

THE team at Treat give their clients the tools, support and guidance to start their own journey towards wellness. With a community of independent practitioners who are truly passionate about holistic health, Treat offers a whole host of therapies – all under one roof. This welcoming collective of highly-skilled therapists, coaches, yogis and massage therapists, offers everything from group sessions, courses and workshops to one-to-one care. Just seven minutes' walk from the city centre, why not Treat yourself today? • *gr*

NESTLED in the historical Cathedral quarter is one of Norwich's hidden gems. Only at Spruce House can you get the signature 'Medi-pedi' – the ultimate in pedicures – as well all manner of maintenance treatments including intimate waxes, lash lifts, nails and a wide range of aesthetic cosmetic and hair treatments. There's resurfacing facials, massages and a body sauna experience too! So why not come in, switch off and indulge in some serious 'sprucing'? • *sh*

Location
4 - 6 Heigham St
NR2 4TE

Location
10 St Martins At Palace Plain
NR3 1RN

Contact
01603 514195
treatnorwich.co.uk

Contact
01603 627527
sprucehouse.co.uk

Soma

Location

-

3 - 6 Bagley's House
Bagley's Court, Pottergate
NR2 1TW

Contact

-

01603 932741
IG @somawellbeingcentre

SOMA is a wellbeing centre/clinic offering alternative therapies and workshop spaces from their newly refurbished and inviting sanctuary in the bustling Norwich Lanes.

Originally designed as a holistic trauma therapy treatment centre, clinic owner Layla Evans specialises in and practices using biodynamic bodywork therapy. The clinic also offers many other complementary therapies ranging from acupuncture, reflexology, natural fertility treatment and various forms of therapeutic bodywork, all of which heal and nurture the mind, body, and soul.

Soma utilises the powerful healing energy of plants: the space is home to many beautiful flora, creating an ambience of peace and tranquility for both those receiving treatments and also the practitioners working there.

For fellow practitioners seeking a beautiful space from which to offer their services, Soma also offers space to book therapy rooms by the day, half day or hourly rate. • *as*

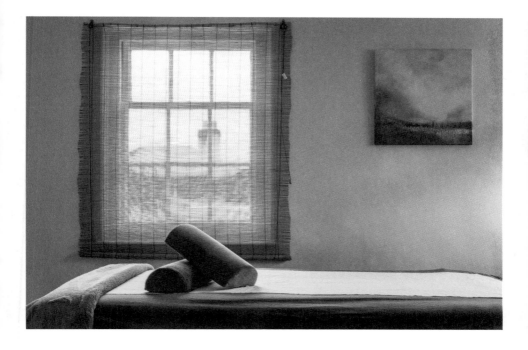

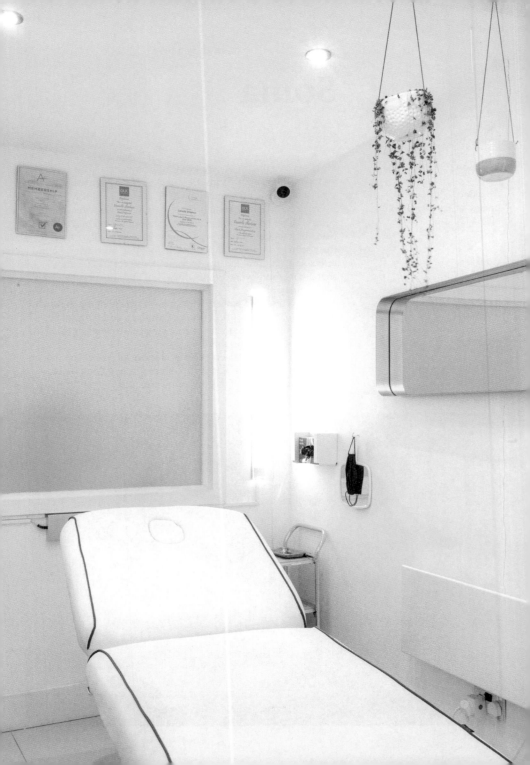

Mae Cosmetics

Location

-

6 St Gregorys Alley
NR2 1ER

Contact

-

maecosmetics.com
IG @maecosmeticsclinic

IF you're looking for a long term solution to boost your self-esteem, Mae Cosmetics has the knowledge, experience and friendliness you need. Mae Cosmetics works in partnership with Nurse Practitioners and Aesthetic Technicians to deliver advanced beauty treatments and aesthetics within a safe and comfortable environment. Treatments include semi-permanent makeup, injectable treatments, skin therapy, body contouring and PDO threads. All are guaranteed to have immediate, long-lasting results with little-to-no-maintenance.

It's important to choose the right clinic for you – and Mae Cosmetics is bound to impress. Rooms are sleek and stylish with lots of beautiful furniture and greenery, and the staff are warm and welcoming. For a snapshot of their real-life transformations, check out Mae Cosmetics on Instagram. • *sm*

Mae Cosmetics Academy

Location

-

6 St Gregorys Alley
NR2 1ER

Contact

-

maecosmetics.com
IG @maecosmeticsclinic

DO you work in beauty and cosmetics? Are you hoping to expand and finesse your skills? We have exciting news! Mae Cosmetics are expanding with the launch of their academy in late 2019, beginning with bespoke training in semi-permanent make up for those looking to further their career within the beauty industry.

The Mae Cosmetics Academy aims to be the hub of all things beauty and cosmetics within Norfolk and the surrounding areas. Subscribe to their social media feeds and keep your eyes peeled on their website for the latest updates.

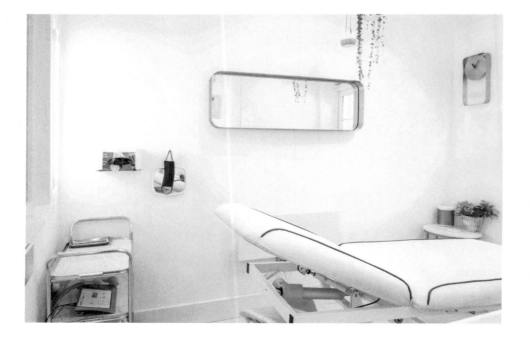

Hoskins Hair

Location

-

76 Upper St Giles St
NR2 1LT

Contact

-

01603 629374
hoskinshair.co.uk

IN the summer of 2014, long-time celebrity London stylist Jamie Hoskins left the Big Smoke to pursue his dream of creating the perfect salon in Norwich...and we're so thankful that he did!

Housed in a beautiful former apothecary's shop on the equally stylish Upper St Giles, the team at Hoskins Hair are on a mission to improve the health and appearance of your hair. Services include a full range of technical colour work, curly hair cutting & styling and Olaplex or On Protection treatments – the ultimate way to repair broken bonds from colour damage. Their pursuit of hair happiness has also led them to partner with Davines, purveyors of naturally-sourced, sustainable hair products from Italy. Perfection! • *sm*

Highball Climbing Centre

Location

-

1 Twickenham Rd
NR6 6NG

Contact

-

01603 513513
highballnorwich.com

HIGHBALL is Norfolk's only dedicated climbing centre, with a vision to provide world-class climbing for all ages and abilities. Climbers have access to 200+ boulder problems and 45+ sport climbing routes – which are regularly changed to keep the walls fresh with new challenges – plus a fully-equipped strength and conditioning area and yoga and pilates classes. Their trained team deliver a full programme of activities, courses and coaching, and organise regular events and local/national climbing competitions, earning a reputation as one of the best centres in the UK.

The social hub of their centre is the BetaCafé; it's plastic free, serving locally-sourced coffee from The Little Red Roaster and Strangers, as well as homemade cakes, food, and wood-fired pizza.

Highball's friendly and supportive crew have created a cool community vibe which resonates with everyone who visits; it's a great place to climb, train or just hang out!

StandenMay

Location

-

1 Magdalen St
NR3 1LE

Contact

-

01603 616396
standenmay.com

FOUNDED by Callum, an award-winning hairdresser, and Paul, a former senior educator for Wella World Studio London, StandenMay reimagines what it is to have your 'hair done'. Influenced by fashion and defined by simply beautiful hair, their Instagram-able salon is inspired by cool-girl hangouts of Miami and London's best hotels, with a laid-back vibe, super luxury service and free Prosecco!

Focusing on bespoke colour and effortless wearability, the colour room set-up is the first of its kind. Whether you're a serial highlighter, annual balayager or regular cut kinda girl (or guy) – experience hair the #STANDENMAYWAY.

The Alignment Collective

The Shiatsu Centre

THE collaborative work of two of Norwich's excellent yoga teachers, The Alignment Collective offers authentic Day and Weekend Yoga Retreats in the heart of Norfolk's countryside. Rose and Sophie bring their deep respect for Yoga and Ayurveda together to create a space in which you can hope to find a greater sense of balance and alignment with yourself. Held at Pensthorpe Nature Reserve and North Norfolk's Tittleshall Barns, their retreats promise to be the perfect tonic for those wishing to escape the bustle of city life. • *sh*

SHIATSU is a form of deeply relaxing holistic bodywork, used to treat a wide range of health conditions. It's great for any stress-related problems and for preventative health care too. Practitioners at the Shiatsu Centre Norwich (the first dedicated Shiatsu clinic in this country) are all highly trained members of The Shiatsu Society UK and provide a friendly and professional service. Other therapies available there include holistic massage, EFT and Qigong healing. The Centre is linked to the Shiatsu College which also offers courses and workshops. • *as*

Location
20A Lower Goat Ln
NR2 1EL

Contact
thealignmentcollective.co.uk
thealignmentcollective@gmail.com

Contact
01603 632555
shiatsucentre.co.uk

Paradox Living

Location

-

Manor Farm Barns
NR14 7PZ

Contact

-

01508 813213
paradoxliving.co.uk

FEELING and looking incredible shouldn't be a hardship. Realising that many people need to take a fresh approach to health and wellbeing, life (and business) partners Evan Beales and Wallis Hubble combined over a decade of experience to form Paradox Living. Paradox treats every client individually, creating a supportive and informative environment to ensure nothing but great results...all they ask from you in return is an open mind about food, exercise and lifestyle habits, and a willingness to prioritise yourself! Leaving their stylish, eco-luxury barn conversion on the outskirts of Norwich, you will be equipped with everything you need to feel energised and happy about your body. • *jr*

Croppers

Location

-

5 St Gregorys Alley
NR2 1ER

Contact

-

01603 623756
IG @croppers 1974

WITH over 40 years' industry experience, Croppers know what it takes to deliver superior customer service. Known for their signature style and comical 'Walkens accepted' sign (inspired by Christopher Walken himself!), this city-centre barber shop is popular with men of all ages. Highly-skilled and always up for a chat, the friendly team at Croppers offer recommended cuts and styles to suit their clients' individual needs. Priding themselves on offering the same warm welcome and attention to detail with each and every customer, Croppers believe it's the people that make the barbering trade what it is today. • *gr*

The Barn Beauty Rooms

Location

-

White House Farm
NR13 6LB

Contact

-

01603 405717
barnbeautyrooms.co.uk

NESTLED away in a lovely little courtyard at White House Farm lies The Barn Beauty Rooms. If you're looking for quiet time out or pampering with a friend, owners Nicci, Alice and their team are here to offer a wide range of beauty and complementary therapies. Treatments in the beautifully-converted barns include Dermaquest facials, Dermaplaning, Neals Yard body treatments, massages, LVL lash lift, reflexology, Bio Sculpture gel nails, microblading, waxing, tinting and more!

The Barn Beauty Rooms is pleased to offer flexible opening hours and free parking six days a week, so you can always find time to squeeze in a much-needed visit. • *sm*

The Gallery Haircutters

Location
-
13 Waterloo Rd
NR3 1EH

Contact
-
01603 787248
IG @thegalleryhaircutters

ESTABLISHED in 1986, The Gallery Haircutters is steeped in expertise with a talented family of 30 stylists. Offering bespoke services such as award-winning colouring, styling and cutting, The Gallery ensures the perfect coiffure with a complimentary consultation offered before your appointment. Situated just north of the city, The Gallery is perfectly poised for residents in NR3, with dedicated parking for those travelling from further afield. Inside, the salon is bright and welcoming and aims to create an ambiently tailored experience for all customers, whilst stylists are trained in all the new techniques to ensure you get the perfect cut, colour and styling. • *sh*

Wits End Pilates

Location

-

13 Grove Avenue
Norwich NR1 2QB

Contact

-

07837 086035
IG @pilatesdotty

WITS END PILATES offer supportive, long-term solutions for those seeking specialist exercise. Rehabilitation, injury, chronic pain and body dysfunction are at the centre of this balance-building exercise program, which uses classical and contemporary forms to correct muscle imbalances. Their friendly personal instructor has 20 years' experience in teaching pilates and personal training, and will work one-to-one with you to make sure that you have the skills to continue a solid home practice – with practical advice given on how to build core strength, stability and mobility. For those wishing to delve deeper, Reiki healing is also offered, ensuring all attendees can balance not only their bodies but also their minds. • *sh*

stay:

38 St Giles

Location

-

38 St Giles St
NR2 1LL

Contact

-

01603 662944
38stgiles.co.uk

FEEL like getting away and cocooning yourself in luxurious Egyptian cotton bedding as you contemplate life's finer moments? 38 St Giles, centrally located near Norwich Market, is a sumptuous five-star boutique bed and breakfast, boasting both history and comfort in its six bedrooms and two suites. Built in 1700, the luxury accommodation features an assortment of period and contemporary furniture and furnishings, including lavish throws and rugs. The staff are welcoming and the rooms, accessed via a grand entry staircase, offer indulgent linens, L'Occitane toiletries and bathrooms with oversized walk-in showers and rainfall showerheads. Look out for the homemade chocolate brownies delivered directly to your room – bliss! • *ar*

Nor–Folk Stays

Location
-
Broads National Park

Contact
-
stays.nor-folk.com
IG @nor_folk_stays

THE WATER CABIN is the first of the Nor–Folk Stays. Adding to their lifestyle journal, shop and creative studio, Nor–Folk (*p213*) have lovingly renovated a 1930's cedar-clad cabin located on the bank of the River Thurne in the heart of the Broads National Park. True to their brand's minimal, paired-back aesthetic, Nor–Folk's Fiona and Bobby have given great consideration to detail at every turn to make their guests' stay as comfortable, relaxing and healing as possible.

The two bedroom cabin (which sleeps four) has a private boat dyke with river frontage, making it an ideal base to explore the Broads by boat, canoe or SUP. With no wifi and a brilliantly-curated collection of inspirational travel and design books and magazines – the Water Cabin encourages you to slow down, unwind and switch off. • *nm*

Maids Head Hotel

Location

-

20 Tombland
NR3 1LB

Contact

-

01603 209955
maidsheadhotel.co.uk

PERFECTLY located in the heart of Norwich, opposite the Cathedral, the historic Maids Head is renowned for being the oldest hotel in the UK. Having recently undergone a multi-million pound refurbishment, the AA 4-star silver hotel boasts 84 uniquely designed bedrooms, along with an AA 2 Rosette WinePress Restaurant. It was proudly named the *EDP*'s Best Independent Hotel in Norfolk and Suffolk 2019, and also deservedly won the Investing in the Future Award.

The WinePress Restaurant features seasonal menus created by Head Chef Magic, a semi-finalist in the National Chef of the Year 2018 competition. He is passionate about sourcing local ingredients from all the fantastic food and drink suppliers in Norfolk and Suffolk.

A warm welcome always awaits at the Maids Head. Relish in an overnight stay, enjoy a traditional afternoon tea in one of the comfortable lounges, relax with friends over dinner, or celebrate with a drink in the Jacobean bar.

Norwich BID is a not-for-profit organisation, funded by local businesses to help make Norwich city centre thrive. VisitNorwich – the destination marketing organisation for Norwich – is part of the BID, and promotes the City of Stories to a local, national and international audience.

supported by

NORWICH UNIVERSITY OF THE ARTS

A specialist university with a forward-thinking approach to arts education, NUA has adapted to the changing worlds of art, design and media with the provision of cutting-edge courses to a student body of over 2,000.

nua.ac.uk

field notes:

credits:

Creative Director
Sam Harrons
IG @samharrons

Directors
Robin Norton
Nick Snell

Head of Design
Joyce Pfeifer
joyceofalltrades.com

Head of Editorial
Steph McKenna
T @stephxmckenna

Head of Photography
Hannah Hutchins
hhutchins.com

Head of Logistics
Ryan Holder

Printer
Steven Pyke
pagebros.co.uk

Photography
Callum Painter
Kelly Simone
Matyáš Paul

Design
Nicole Mitchell
George Wheadon

Writers
Caitlin Bone *cb*
Joe Collier *jc*
Emma-Jane Corsan *ejc*
Lizzy Guy *lg*
Poppy Hammond *ph*
Sara Harrington *sh*
James MacDonald *jm*
Thomas Markham-Uden *tmu*
Steph McKenna *sm*
Nicole Mitchell *nm*
Jordane Roberts *jr*
Georgina Rouse *gr*
Alyssa Russo *ar*
Alysia Schuetzle *as*
Fin Slater *fs*
Cathy White *cw*
Ellie White *ew*

Contributors
Chloe Baker-Cooper
Evangeline Hallett
Thomas Markham-Uden
Yvonne Popplewell
Georgina Rouse

Image Credits
Steve Adams *p289*
Joseph Barrett *p268*
Fiona Burrage *p146*, *p148*,
p212 - 213, *p250*, *p326 - 327*
A J Digital *p188 - 189*
Kev Foster *p78 - 79*
Alex Game *p173*
Tristan Holden *p298 - 299*
Fran Kennedy *p280 - 281*
Adam Maizey *p186 - 187*
Benjamin Mathers *p195*, *p263*
Jo Millington *p198*
Amy Ollett *p202 (right)*
RMS *p94 - 95*
Andi Sapey *p182*, *p214 (right)*,
p217 (right)

SHHHH Guide to Norwich
Published by SHHHH Collective Limited

Connect with us
Instagram: @shhhh.norwich
Facebook: /shhhhguide

Show your support for independent
businesses and connect with like-minded
locals by using the hashtags:
#shhhhnorwich
#norwichnatives

Become a stockist
Get in touch via the website
www.shhhh.co.uk

Contribute and Feedback
We encourage feedback and welcome
content ideas from all of our readers.
Message us via our social media or email us
via the website if you have a suggestion or
would like to get involved.

Printed by
Page Bros Limited, Norwich, England

ISBN 978-1-5272-4417-7

G . F
SMITH
1885 ONWARDS

Cover
Colorplan Marrs Green
270gsm with Pebble Emboss.

Pages
Munken Design Polar Smooth
100gsm

gfsmith.com